Reflections
on Caring for
an Aging Parent

Reflections
on Caring for
an Aging Parent

Audrey Brown Lightbody

Chalice Press
St. Louis, Missouri

All scripture quotations, unless otherwise indicated, are from the *New Revised Standard Version Bible*, copyright 1989, Division of Christian Education of the National Council of the Churches of Christ in the USA. Used by permission.

"In the Bulb, There Is a Flower," words by Natalie Sleeth. © 1986 Hope Publishing Co., Carol Stream, IL 60188. All rights reserved. Used by permission.

Excerpt reprinted with permission of Manisses Communications Group, Inc., 208 Governor St., Providence, RI 02906. *Provide Residents with the Best Attention*, Long Term Care Quality Letter, vol. 6, no. 21, p. 7. Reproduced by permission of the publisher via Copyright Clearance Center, Inc.

Cover: Mark Edwards
Interior design: Elizabeth Wright
Art direction: Michael Domínguez

This book is printed on acid-free, recycled paper.

Visit Chalice Press on the World Wide Web at
www.chalicepress.com

10 9 8 7 6 5 4 3 2 1   99 00 01 02 03 04

Library of Congress Cataloging–in–Publication Data

Lightbody, Audrey Brown.
     Reflections on caring for an aging parent / by Audrey Brown Lightbody.
          p.   cm.
     ISBN 0-8272-3220-9
     1. Aging parents–United States–Family relationships.   2. Aging parents–Care–United States. 3. Lightbody, Audrey Brown Correspondence. 4. Mothers and daughters–United States Case studies. 5. Adult children–United States Correspondence.
     I. Title.
HQ1064.U5L555 1999
306.874'3 — dc21   99-38526
                                                                CIP

Printed in the United States of America

*This book is lovingly dedicated
to the memory of my mother,
—the woman she was for much of my lifetime,
the woman she became when disabilities occurred—
both of whom were valued and loved by me.*

Contents

Acknowledgments

I am grateful for the sustaining presence of my husband, who lived through so much of the trauma of the daily care for my mother and who was a support through the times of putting this material together.

I wish to acknowledge three persons who helped to bring this book to life by giving their wise insights into the best manner in which to present this material: Dr. William Clements, whose assistance was from the beginning; Dr. Philip Anderson, who helped me to look at my material in a slightly different way; and Dr. Lester McAllister, who was instrumental in my finding a publisher. To each of them I offer my sincere gratitude.

I need to mention the wonderful care and support offered on a daily basis by the staff of the Health Services Center at Pilgrim Place in Claremont, California, where Mother lived for the last four years of her life. Their constant caring helped me to find meaningful ways of looking after her in her disabled state. They were a wonderful resource. I wish that all persons who deal with family members with disabilities could have such kind helpers.

A special word of appreciation to my editor, Dr. David Polk at Chalice Press, for his encouragement, valuable advice, and continuing presence until this book was completed.

Preface

Somehow it seems impossible to think anyone can be interested in reading, let alone writing, another book on coping with the problems of the elderly and having to parent a senior parent. That is, however, what this book is about—caring for one's own aging parent.

In these letters, journal entries, and reflections, I share the story of a challenging but loving relationship with one person with multiple disabilities, what the aging process has done, its ramifications for this person, for the family, and the community of which she is part. It is important to see individuals as separate and distinct entities; to know that they were and are whole people, no matter what their afflictions. Perhaps such an understanding will allow the reader to step back and objectively analyze how best to make these growing-old years into joyful times of loving communion and communication with an aging parent.

There is no sense in which this book will speak to all aging persons except as we are all part of that human condition. Growing old is such a differing scenario for all of us. For some the appearance of old age happens early; for others it just creeps up on us, and we come to recognize at a much later time all those little clues we should have seen and acted on much earlier, thus making the whole process more difficult than need be.

I have written this book on a very personal level. It is a retired person's individualized response to living and dealing with an aging parent who has progressively lost hearing and sight, with the additional ramification of dementia and hallucinatory images caused by severe sensory deprivation, plus the addition of new physical disabilities. It is my hope that in this book real people may be seen, real human beings, as well as the problems and conditions that have developed over the years.

This is a book written about my mother and her problems as a person with multiple disabilities. I will attempt to share my understanding of a variety of situations and will point out the difficulties, as well as some of my own peculiar answers learned through the daily trial and error method of coping. In these pages I will share very real feelings—responses containing within them the seeds of disappointment, apathy, sympathy, loss of hope, anger, love, and many other emotional byways. Breaking this down into the various kinds of disabilities allows me to focus on each part and yet, with it all, I hope that the sense of the whole perspective will never be lost.

This book is written in two parts. The beginning and ending are written as though they were pages in a personal diary and contain my reflections on how I experienced the role reversal of becoming a "parent" to my own mother. The central section contains a group of letters written to her and deals specifically with everyday time with my mother.

I wrote these letters to my mother during the time she was alive. But even then I recognized that I could never send the letters to her because of all her limitations. However, my mother has since died, and now it is a reality that these letters can never be sent. They will appear to be written to a living person, and so they were. There is no sense that this book is a how-to for others, but it has within its pages a catharsis for my own doubts and frustrations. I hope it may strike some resonant chord with others who deal on an almost daily level with an aging parent who has become the child.

Journaling My Insights

Lord,
it's only me,
pursuing something I'm not sure of.

It's only me,
looking for a road map. Or a set of rules.

I like things clear cut and specific, Lord.
And when you ask me to accept "on faith,"
you ask a hard thing.
What is faith anyway,
but committing myself to something I'm not sure of?

All of which is further complicated, Lord, when I find out
how many of the things that I am sure of aren't so...

But I'll settle, Lord, for this growing awareness,
and count myself rich indeed.
Amen, amen.[1]

I begin my story of learning to parent a parent with selected pages from my diary. They are written without dates because I wanted only to put down those ideas, those thoughts, those ponderings that came through to me even as I dealt with all the trauma and moments of those last years of Mother's life. These written-down thoughts were always part of the parenting process, a necessary adjunct to the times of Mother's life. My first entries have to do with my decision to write the letters, and then they move on to the ideas churned up within me as I spent time with the concerns raised by being a parent to my parent.

Thinking about My Feelings

My letters will recount all the trauma, the moments of despair, the moments of joy and gladness—which have been few and far between—but here in these pages I come to the time of trying to sum up my own feelings, what I have learned, and how I have dealt with these cares and concerns. It is only fitting that this be done in the form of letters in a diary, written by a cognitively aware person who knows about being the caregiver, the parent, the person aching to improve matters for the parent/child.

Mother's multiple disabilities have caused stress and pain for both of us. As I tried to think about the stress in my life due to parenting my parent, I turned to the book *Living with the Disabled* and found this telling statement:

> Stress is really a condition of life. Only death relieves an individual of all stress. Although we have little control over most of the stress we encounter in life, we do have a choice in how to cope with it. We can regard emotional stress as an opportunity for personal growth, just as an athlete uses physical stress to strengthen his body. Successfully coping with a stressful event gives us new abilities and a sense of accomplishment. On the other hand, we can let stress abuse us, so that we feel helpless and anxious.[2]

In these diary writings I want to discuss only what the effects of stress have been on me; Mother's problems will be enumerated in my letters. I hope that by noting the stresses I may also discover new ways of coping and help my personal growth.

Thinking about the pain caused by Mother's disabilities, I came upon this statement from Rainer Maria Rilke that gives this valuable insight into pain:

So you must not be frightened...if a sadness rises up before you larger than any you have ever seen; if a restiveness, like light and cloud-shadows, passes over your hands and over all you do. You must think that...life has not forgotten you, that it holds you in its hands; it will not let you fall. Why do you want to shut out of your life any agitation, any pain, any melancholy, since you really do not know what these states are working upon you? Why do you want to persecute yourself with the question whence all this may be coming and whither it is bound?...Just remember that sickness is the means by which an organism frees itself of foreign matter; so one must just help it to be sick, to have its whole sickness and break out with it, for that is its progress...You must be patient as a sick man...There are in every illness many days when the doctor can do nothing but wait. And this it is that you, insofar as you are your own doctor, must now above all do.[3]

Looking at Mother's disability as an illness that I have, and will continue to experience, may serve as a pathway to new challenges if I can find the ability to meet these tests within myself. Will it have any potential to assist me as a caregiver to lead my mother to new growth?

These diary writings, containing stress, pain, illness, and disability, serve as a summing up of my insights. The summing up of anything—a play, a music score, a document—should be a tying together of all the loose threads that have been part of what has gone before. In happy-ending stories all those disparate pieces blend and merge together to make the perfect conclusion. However, not all stories end with all the pieces conforming in perfect unity, nor does all music conclude on a triumphant sustained high, nor does life fit into the perfect mold.

My ruminations and soul-searching may more resemble a still unfinished piece of work in progress than a finale.

Contained within my ruminations are all the dangling threads, the bits and pieces of what has happened in two lives. Since this is real life, and it is difficult to see a pattern in an unfinished piece, there will be no clearly defined motif. To attempt to create a pattern where none exists would be false. I know that for me the varied pieces contain the whole and that they are uniquely real, as all persons' lives and perceptions are uniquely real. Does this ending show the way to a future as yet unrevealed? Will it change two lives? I do not know the answer, but I have hope that I may be more keenly aware of what I must do in these circumstances. My diary letters will contain my thinking at this moment in time and space.

Thinking about My Feelings of Anger and Resentment

I know that the hardest part of our relationship in this time is Mother's inability to believe any reassuring words I may offer. I was telling friends about my frustration of ever convincing her that I was believable. They said, "I am sure that this must hurt you and cause you great pain." I reflected on those words and realized that hurt was not the emotion I felt.

In my own mind, I have been able to separate the words that my mother says about not believing me into something that is coming from a person different from the one I have known from childhood. Mother is no longer that person. It is almost as if when her paranoia and delusions took over she became someone unrelated to all that had gone before in our relationship.

I am aware, however, that I do have strong emotions related to all this. I find myself frustrated, oh so frustrated, and angry and resentful. It takes so much out of me to attempt to find ways of making her feel secure. I am angry that I have not been able to remove those grievous fears from her mind. When I come from visiting her, I know that my frustration level has reached its zenith, and I dislike not only how I feel, but how it makes me react to her.

When this happens, I need to find some way to let off some of the steam that accumulates within me. Walking is an excellent outlet—sometimes it requires a lot of walking! I constantly need to remind myself that I am not talking with or trying to help a lucid human being—that I am not working with a cognitive mother. These feelings are so devastating that it might be easier to live with "hurt." How do I shrug off what it means to have a delusional mother, when for years I only knew a logical, clear-thinking person?

I wonder if opening up these feelings helps me to put them into perspective. Will thinking about my own agonizing concerns, as well as the exasperation I feel when I have to try to make Mother feel less insecure, become a cure-all for these negative feelings? I know better than to believe that.

These resentments, angers, and frustrations impact our relationship. I know this is true from my side of the equation. I wish Mother could share her feelings, but if she could, then my need to explode about these concerns would disappear because, once again, she would be a rational human being.

I miss the mother for whom I could bring words of reassurance. I want to find whatever will bring release from the gnawing anxieties that beset her. I am at a total loss to know how to do anything worthwhile with all the emotions that are part of our relationship. In spite of Mother's being a different person, and in spite of my feelings of anger, resentment, and frustration, I want love to flow in both directions and for us to surmount these difficulties.

No Answers

In the never-to-be-sent letters that follow, I reflect on the variety of concerns I have faced and on my feelings. I have tried to put myself in my mother's place, I have been subjective and objective, and I have asked others to give me their insights. I realize that over and over again in my

5

letters, I keep repeating, "There is no answer." All of these avenues have only led me to the same dead end.

The other day in a book I was reading, these words about mystery, even though they were used about an entirely different subject, resonated with me:

> By "mystery" I do not mean temporary ignorance that will later be swept away by additional information, or questions that will someday be resolved by future research. I mean mystery in the strongest possible sense—something unknowable, something essentially beyond human understanding.[4]

While I do not equate my concerns as being beyond human understanding, I do realize that I am dealing with a mystery that is too profound for me; indeed, it is beyond my understanding. I am seeking insight and knowledge, and they are not there.

In that same book these words about "The Pathless Path" from Gertrude Stein sum up how I am feeling at this point:

> There is no answer.
> There never has been an answer.
> There never will be an answer.
> That's the answer.[5]

I know that at some future date there may be answers, but I am not certain how useful and valid they will be in my situation. I keep thinking that I am missing something. How I wish that would be true. It is terribly depressing to think that the life of one whom I hold so very dear will be snuffed out in a less than joyful way because I have no answers.

Since there are no sure ways, no paths to follow where others have led the way, no simple solution to lift the pall of darkness, silence, and dementia, I must strike out in journeyings that will be uniquely my own, even as our relationship is unique to us.

My quest for answers seems a little like the knights of old seeking the Holy Grail. Each of the knights involved in the search looked in different places, found varying clues, and had his own roadway to search out. I suspect that there are others out there, looking at different problems, who are attempting to find answers for assisting loved ones to achieve growth and find meaning even through the hardships of debilitating health. We are a host of people lost without a road map, seeking surcease from our aimless wanderings through answers that do not satisfy, that are not helpful. "No answers" is my anguished cry! "No answers" is our cry of pain!

I would like to turn these cries into a dawning of new hope. I saw the daylight this morning with its fingers of red slashed across the sky that foretold of a beautiful new day offering the promise of fair skies and sunshine and open vistas for new adventures. All this spoke to me, telling me that, even though I do not have answers, I can find little rays of light that may help to illuminate the darkness of "no answers" and open up a brighter day for today and possibly for future days. Maybe I don't need the permanent answers. Maybe I just need to find the little moments that change "no answers" into joy for this one period of time. Is this my quest—to find answers just for today?

Laughter

One of the things I have learned during these five years of dealing with Mother's dementia is the importance of a sense of humor and the value of laughter. I know that I need the release that only laughter can give from the heavy burden of trying to deal with the needs that arise out of her unconscious.

It is fascinating to watch the convoluted thought and to wonder what in Mother's past experience could bring to the forefront of her mind such inane situations. Stories that have come from Mother's fragmented mind are truly hilarious, beating any soap opera ever created. I recognize a fertile, creative mind at work, but unfortunately it is at work on unreality. Shamelessly, I have told some of my friends the stories of life as mother has related them to me. Together we have shared laughter over the impossibility of those stories. I hope as I share Mother's inventive tales that my friends do not think that I am laughing at my mother, but only at her demented hallucinations and quirky events.

Laughter is also something that I need to pass on to Mother. How grim her days must seem to her, separated from all meaningful contact. I can see her sitting alone, apparently with no thoughts in her mind, but know, in fact, that she ponders those weird, fanciful, unhumorous thoughts. I wish I knew some way to overcome her fanciful demons and give her the healing that laughter brings. Perhaps if she could laugh more, the grim difficulties that obsess her personally and get transferred to an imaginary friend would disappear

I know that I must make a greater effort to laugh with her, but even after all these years I do not know how to do that. We both pay the price of her insecurity because of our inability to make connections with humor and laughter. Trying to bring laughter in simple ways may bring a smiling mouth, but the gleam in the eye that once was there is missing. I wish she could hear adequately so that I could tell her jokes or stories that would produce deep belly-laughs. It is so frustrating to want to *do* something, when I must settle for both of us just *being*. I want that being to be filled with fun and laughter and close relationship, but it isn't. Will it ever be possible to change grimness into glee?

Dancing

There I was, sitting in church, listening to the pastor's prayer, when I was suddenly jolted, enough that I opened my eyes, when she said something about finding ways to sing and dance and clap before the Lord. It made me lose all sense of the prayer because I was taken back to Psalm 30:10–12.

Hear, O LORD, and be gracious to me!
    O LORD, be my helper!

You have turned my mourning into dancing;
    you have taken off my sackcloth
    and clothed me with joy,

so that my soul may praise you and not be silent.

O LORD my God, I will give thanks to you
forever.

It hit me like a thunderbolt—that's what I want for
my mother—to turn her mourning into dancing! I want
her to be able to praise and not be silent!

I almost had to laugh as I expanded on the idea—my
mother dancing? Mother grew up in a rigid churchgoing
family in the early years of the twentieth century. Dancing was not one of the things "good Christians" did,
anymore than they wore makeup or worked on Sunday.
Never would they have danced before the Lord! Mother
never knew the joy of putting her body into motion and
in time with the music to offer a hymn of praise and delight with carefree abandon. Swooping and soaring and
feeling airborne, instead of being grounded, never found
expression in her understanding of joy. And yet that is what
I wish I could do for her.

Her fragile body, her shuffling steps, her fear of falling, and now her wheelchair confinement preclude this
avenue of literal joyous freedom. Mother seems locked into
her mourning and her silence. What can I do to shake the
lethargy of a body mired in such groundedness and disability? Is it possible for me to create flights of fancy that
will lift her spirits so that she can dance—if only in her
mind?

I wonder if *I* am too firmly attached to earthbound
realities, so that I dare not allow my imagination to soar to
new heights of joyous freedom. Must I learn to find new
forms myself before I can be Mother's instructor? I am
plagued with so many questions, so many doubts. These

keep me like a wallflower, unwilling and afraid to move away from groundedness into the airiness of the dance. Perhaps I need to forget all the inane, trivial conversations and dare to plow new furrows to be filled with joy and hope. How do I begin to break the chains that hold me to "safe" ways of dealing with Mother's multiple problems? If I want to create the opportunity for the dance, there are some givens: It will not happen in just one hour, just one day; I must first try out my wings; it will be difficult, if not impossible, to help Mother put on dancing shoes, because the will must be there to persevere, as well as the belief that dancing will improve life and offer opportunities for growth. I want my mother to laugh and clap and dance. I want to laugh and clap and dance with her in these twilight years of hers. I hope I may have the patience and the reliance on God to lead me into my own dance of joy that will be reflected in mother's movement from silence to praise.

Changes/Growth—for Mother

It is almost unreal the way that some of my recent reading is like a touchstone to my inner thinking and to our situation. As I deliberated on what this time in Mother's life should be, I came across these words in a book about long-term care facilities:

> Change is an electrifying and unnerving process that requires the persistent application of energy. Given this, it is easy to see why people are so reluctant to surrender the habits and routines that make their world a comfortable, understandable place in which to live.[6]

This certainly applies to Mother. There have been so many changes in her life, demanding constant adjustment. Her energy level has plummeted to the nadir level; neither is Mother happy, even though she is in a controlled environment that should allow her to relax and feel secure. Something seems to keep moving her to find new means of expression, and that is unnerving for both of us.

The words from *The Eden Alternative* raise serious questions for me:

> First we must recognize, appreciate and promote each resident's capacity for growth...It is much harder to accept [this] as true for the severely demented and disabled. The truth is that no human being has completely lost the capacity for growth, no matter how small or how obscure, until the last breath is drawn.[7]

I assume that Mother is seeking some path that will lead to fulfillment, but I do not know how to find that path or how to show her the way. My telling her that there is nothing I can do to alleviate an intolerable situation leads to the response by her, "Well, at least you could be sympathetic." Her requirements for "being sympathetic" almost guarantee that anything I say will not be adequate, even if I make an effort to remedy the situation. How can I create growth opportunities when my own poverty of resources gives no answers? Of course, I am the person determining what will mean growth for my mother. Perhaps growth for her will be merely finding serenity in her present surroundings, finding moments of joy, recognizing the love and compassion that surround her. Growth may be exchanging her wilderness or desert experiences of awful isolation for a rain forest of love, new adventures that can happen in her mind, and joy in simple things shared— like just sitting in my home in fellowship with the family. Perhaps I can find ways in which to give word pictures that will sustain her inner world. I guess I need to work on that. I want to try to find selfless ways to ensure happy years that may be intimations of immortality. I think it is worth a shot!

Change and Growth Revisited

Today was a day of griping and inordinate demands; a day when I thought I just could not take any more.

Today was a time when I almost felt abused. Some of my never-to-be-sent letters reflect that feeling. I wish I could retract those words, even though they accurately reflect my feelings on given occasions.

In some reading I have been doing lately, these statements from *Living with the Disabled* resonate with what I sense has occurred in our lives.

> Any change in our normal living patterns will cause stress...Changes can occur when a family member becomes disabled; they cause stress because they threaten our personal security and accustomed patterns of living...

> Faced with the threats that disability presents, we can choose to fight by attacking what seems to be the cause of the problem...or we can flee. We can abandon or ignore our relative...

> Disability in our family tends to inspire feelings of fear, anger, frustration, guilt, and depression. All of these feelings are normal, but their focus is not always appropriate...When involved in caring for a disabled relative, we experience many inappropriate feelings.[8]

I must acknowledge that I suffer from all those feelings and recognize that many of them are inappropriate. When I think about the threats that disability presents, I know that I am unable to abandon or ignore Mother. My daily visits consume significant amounts of time, but seldom do I find them joyous occasions. Is the ungenerous giving of my time a way in which I choose to flee from the onerous demands? Should annoyance show because Mother seems so unwilling to accept her myriad disabilities? Even with all these questions, I know that I must be there for her. Abandonment is not an option; therefore, I realize I must change, but I just don't know how to refocus.

I keep coming across readings that make me feel as if I must do more.

Agents of effective change are able to communicate a clearly defined and apparently reasonable alternative to the status quo...Effective change is always accompanied by a palpable sense of urgency.[9]

I most certainly am not an agent of effective change, because I have discovered that I have no clearly defined alternatives at all, nor do I have a sense of urgency. When old age and a deteriorating body are the primary causes of the problems, and the secondary causes are creations of the mind, there is little that can be done to alleviate any one or all of the causes. I am powerless to change these conditions, and so are those with the proper technical skills. Since I recognize all of these facts, the achievement of growth and giving Mother a comfortable place to be seem to be lost causes.

Just as I began to feel comfortable with myself, I found this other reading:

When we dedicate ourselves to helping other people grow, our work must be defined by their needs and capacities, not ours...Care is selfless. It must be guided by the capacities and needs of the person being cared for.[10]

It was then that I discovered I am not selfless! My current commitment is really only to take care of her, not to try to achieve growth. I do not know how to help her achieve growth, especially because of all the changes to be found in Mother at this point in her life. What I need to consider is what changes *I* need to make to promote both her growth and my own.

On Writing Letters

The common problem—yours, mine, everyone's—
Is not to fancy what were fair in life
Provided it could be; but finding first
What may be, then find how to make it fair
Up to our means—a very different thing![11]

Writing letters is one of the means by which we inform, share important news, send thank-you's for gifts given to us, seek to bring solace in times of death or illness. It is a way of telling history—the story of what happens in our lives. Being a written word, letters have a solidity about them not found in the spoken word. Written words form a frame of reference that can be looked back on and be the context for what will come next.

Using letters as the means of telling a story has been used frequently by authors and dramatists. There has even been a play entitled *Love Letters*, using an interesting device—only two people who read love letters aloud. The part that is intriguing is that the play continues for numbers of weeks in a theater, but each twosome changes after a brief period. If one saw the performance by one set of actors, one could wonder how the same script would be handled by another set of actors. Would the same stresses be heard, the same values given as the scenes are portrayed by different people? It is a very definitive way of gaining perspective.

15

These letters of mine will tell a particular story—a story of aging disabilities and what happens in two people's lives. The stresses and perspective that the reader brings to these letters will determine their validity for each person. For me, as the writer of the letters, they are very real and are, in fact, my story.

In these letters telling of the journey of two people, there is a history of real disabilities, but even more a sense of the feelings, the despair, the hope, all those emotions that go into the present life of a mother and daughter. There is, contained within these letters, my "how to" parent my parent.

Dear Mother,

Today I came back from visiting with you after your second broken hip (the same one). I got to the hospital in time to give all the relevant information, acting as your attorney in fact, and confirmed all my intuitions that I had indeed become your parent. I really feel the need to share with you what being a parent's parent is all about, even though it is in no way unique.

Given that in this moment you are so dependent on me, you might think we could talk about this and thus create a better understanding of the dynamics of our situation. However, I know and believe that even in your best moments *you* know that this is impossible. Your blindness, deafness, and unacknowledged dementia prevent lucid, logical conversation. So, this becomes the first letter among many that never will be sent, but they will lift up my desire to share with you my perceptions about what has happened, and continues to occur, in our interactions in the present and will also inform whatever future there is between the two of us.

To attempt to do in letters what even in your early retirement years we could do in conversation or argument or confrontation is a daunting task. The letters will only be one-sided, and, while I may assume your responses, basically all I am doing is giving one set of perceptions—mine. There will be no dialogue. There can be no words

from you—of disputation or affirmation. Thus, this becomes my attempt to deal with the difficulties and joys of being your parent-daughter as you finish your closing years caught in a world with no windows to the outside world.
I love you,
Audrey

Dear Mother,
When I started writing these letters to you, I thought all I needed to do was just talk about our interactions, our relationships, and how I view what has happened to you in these latter years when you are no longer the vital, rational person I have always known. However, I have discovered that other people's experiences, as found in the literature of our time, give me a clearer understanding of your patterns. This information is like road signs along the way to give me assurance that the route taken is not too far off the mark.

I know I cannot become totally dependent on these markings, because each person's journey is different. How you and I have interacted or how I respond on my own is part of the sum total of our individual journeyings as well as those places where our lives have intersected. The markers, the road signs, are important as a check against my remembered actions.

Putting all this into a letter to you assumes that, if I were to send these letters, you, out of your vital years, would relate to what I say in them and want to have the same guidelines to understand where all this leads. That dichotomy between your previous life and what you now experience is exactly what these letters are about.

I know my letters and the incidental information are really written to the mother who no longer exists; that is why they will never be sent. I grieve for that loss and wish that I could share so much more with you.
I love you,
Audrey

Letters to My Mother Regarding Hearing Problems

Grant me the gift of telling you my grief.
I shall not voice it often, for I know
Entrenchment of the widely-held belief
That bravery requires scars must not show.
But if you are my friend, please understand
My need to tell you of this devastation.
I will learn silence, but your ear and hand
Just now could start a healing consolation.[12]

Hearing Aids

Dear Mother,

Today, again, was one of those days when you called me from the nursing home to tell me that your hearing aid was not working. It was so difficult to get information to you over the phone, since you could not hear what I was saying. I told the nurse to have you start talking, assume I was there, and then after you finished to take the phone back so that I could give her the necessary information. Even that did not work, so I left home immediately to come over. I first checked to make sure that the battery was working, and it was. Then I tried the adjustment for sound and pushed the other switch from phone connection to regular hearing, and it worked. There was no real problem, only that you were pushing the wrong lever on the hearing aid. This was something that a nurse could have done, but you seem to feel that I am the only one who can handle the hearing aid problems.

I really do not understand why you will not let the nursing staff assist you when problems arise. You say, "They don't know anything about adjusting it or putting in batteries." They do it for many of the other patients, so I guess this is just one way of trying to maintain your independence and sense of control.

Whenever there is a hearing aid problem you become frantic and almost impossible to deal with. I know that such difficulties could mean that your very tenuous relationship with the outside world would be totally cut off— and that is too awful for you to contemplate. It is an equally horrible thought for me. I guess I do not know what either of us would do if even your limited hearing was gone. What communication would we be able to have other than just touch? Would touch be enough, or would you then feel as if you were in a deserted place, lost to contact with the world? If I think these thoughts, what must go through your mind? You are frantic, but I must remain calm and see if there is some way that I can resolve the problem. Therefore, I cannot even begin to deal with the deeper ramifications of such a loss.

The hearing aid is really a symbol of our communication skills. When it is working well and you are hearing at your best level, when I can reach you because I take the time to speak slowly and in a modulated tone, then we are at one with each other. Without the hearing aid, our abilities are truncated almost to the impossible. Oh, how I hope that you can retain enough hearing power that we may communicate with each other until the end of your days.

I love you,
Audrey

Batteries

Dear Mother,

Buying batteries for your hearing aid is something that you never seem to feel I can remember to do correctly. I have been buying them for you for at least eight years, and every time you question whether I will buy the right size batteries (13E is indelibly engraved on my memory). I even know the best place to get such batteries, but longevity at doing this service doesn't seem to count for anything with you. I still get the usual questions. Is this, too, a means of trying to keep control?

I really hate to have you go with me to buy the batteries, but sometimes you need them at the time that I am taking you out for other things. Then we have to have that hassle over battery size at the counter in the drugstore. It always seems that this is the time when your hearing is at its poorest, and I cannot get through to you that I am holding the correct battery. I try to speak so that you can hear, and salespersons come rushing over to find out if there is a problem. I hasten to explain that you have a major hearing loss and that everything is all right, but, Mother, you look so distraught that I am certain they feel that I am abusing you. Such times are strictly lose–lose situations and I want to hide away. Since you cannot see well or hear, the resulting situation has no "squirm" effect on you, but, oh how much I just want to slink away. I really prefer to get the batteries on my own.

I went over to visit you just the other day, and I knew you were not hearing, but you insisted you could hear just fine. However, you were not understanding anything that was being said. I took out your hearing aid and discovered that the battery was dead. I simply put in another battery, and then we were able to really communicate. I wonder what it was that made you think you were hearing me.

The batteries themselves are so little, but they take up an extraordinary amount of my time and cause many difficulties. I guess this will be an ongoing concern.

I love you,

Audrey

Hearing Aids Again

Dear Mother,

I remember the time last week when your hearing aid went out completely, and I had to get you to the audiologist. The needed repairs meant that you would be without it for ten days. Fortunately, I keep another hearing aid at home, along with a supply of the kind of batteries needed for its use. This hearing aid, left over from the time when you used two aids, is not as useful, but nevertheless workable. It was a simple matter to attach your ear mold to it and thus give you back your hearing during this repair period. Since this aid requires different batteries, I cannot let you keep them, for you will only get them mixed up with your current batteries, and so I make arrangements for the nursing station to have the batteries. Of course, I am not sure that you will ask for them, even when I tell you they have them.

In going for the repairs, I remembered all the appointments and the training you went through to get to this point in your hearing odyssey. Way back when I was in high school, you first began to say that you could not hear well in one ear, and so you always tried to sit so that people were on your good side. You dealt with the hearing problem in that way for a long, long time. You went through all the denials that most people suffer because it was so difficult to admit to others and to yourself that you could not hear. It wasn't until your retirement years that you sought out advice and discovered that you had nerve deafness that is irreversible. There wasn't much that could be done about it except use hearing aids.

Your first hearing aid made such a difference for you. There was only one hearing aid on the ear that was still functioning, even if poorly. Later in time you tried using two hearing aids even though there was no hearing in the left ear, and for a while you seemed to do better. The hearing loss deepened, and so you took lip reading classes. I was so proud of the way that you learned this well enough to teach those classes for other persons with hearing problems.

Your refusal to give up on finding ways to improve your communication skills resulted in an appointment with one of the country's leading ear specialists, who said there was nothing more that could be done. The operations that might have been helpful were not possibilities for you.

If trying over and over and over again with all the new technological advances, all the training skills, and seeking always to enhance your ability to communicate were all that it took, then you would be a hearing person. That is not the situation, and so here you are today hearing in such a limited fashion. I recognize that it isn't that you cannot hear people talking, but that you have no idea of what it is they say or what the sounds mean. I know there are days when you could scream because nothing makes any sense. You keep yourself at such a high pitch of endeavor, and it counts for nothing.

I do admire your stick-to-it-iveness, this quality that stood you in good stead in your younger years when life was easier. Now that you are so dependent on others' doing things for you, this same quality sometimes drives me to distraction. I have accepted that there is really nothing more that can be done, and I know you have as well, and yet, there is something that makes you keep trying for more. If I should have the same problem, how would I cope with it? Would I accept it placidly, or would I rail against what life has done to me? I know that you are so downcast that life has little meaning, and I realize that when you have put so much energy into trying to improve your life, you must feel totally defeated. I resent for you that there is nothing more that can be done.

I love you,
Audrey

Equipment for the Hard of Hearing

Dear Mother,

Your incessant desire to find ways around your hearing losses led us to seek a great number of items that might permit you to be part of the hearing world. We scoured all kinds of publications that had articles about people with hearing problems and contained advertisements of inventions and equipment that related to hearing loss. We certainly tried too many of these; some worked well and were helpful, but some of them were beyond your ability to cope with them at the time you purchased them.

When you could no longer hear your TV, we bought a closed captioning machine. This valuable instrument turned those programs having closed captioning into the opportunity for you to read what was being said audibly. The audio part of the program became a visual experience. The closed captioning ran along the bottom of the screen, and we learned that it really required all of one's attention to follow the words. While it made TV a pleasure again, the close attention it demanded was very enervating as well.

Listening for the phone became a major concern. You were in a constant state of uneasiness lest you miss some calls. The simple device that could be hooked up to the phone that would turn a light on when the phone was ringing was a godsend. What a boon this was for you, and for us, because we knew that you could recognize that a call was coming in. We resolved the problem of what to do about the light when you were in bed in another room by simply moving the lamp around the corner.

A telephone provided by A T &T with hearing amplification built into the phone itself provided a solution to the more difficult problem of being able to hear the caller. Then we had to cope with whether or not you should keep your hearing aids in, in addition to the amplified phone. As your hearing became progressively worse, none of these devices were able to work for you. Then we had to think of other solutions.

Another welcome invention was the small microphone/receiver set that could be hung around the neck of the person speaking, allowing for amplification through the receiver. This worked quite well, but you took a dislike to it and refused to use it even when the rest of the family found it helpful. A few years later, the audiologist introduced you to a similar device that could be plugged into your hearing aid. It had a small microphone that could be used in large gatherings that would give you keener hearing. You used this for a short period of time at church services and when the family was gathered together. It was more effective, but then you also gave that up. I remember how irritated all of us were that you were unwilling to make the effort to use this tool that might assist you. I think now that all these things came too late for you. Your hearing loss was too advanced, and your discrimination was almost gone. The effort required demanded too much of you. We hoped that the instruments themselves would serve you in the ways we desired. We all wanted you to have meaning in your life, but on our terms. How little we understood the frustrations that you experienced, and how devastating each loss was for you. How insensitive we were at recognizing your inability to cope with the demands that all these technical advances required. Forgive us, forgive me for the lack of understanding.

I wonder if your refusal to make the best use of this equipment had nothing to do with the time frame in which it occurred. Perhaps your refusals were another way of maintaining control of various situations. Did you reject this help because you would have to struggle with what we were attempting to say, and it was too much effort? If you did not hear what the family was talking about, would you then be able to take charge of the conversation? Maybe it was a little of both. I know how important control is for you—does it affect this hard of hearing time as well? Even with advanced equipment we did not make significant progress in giving you the assistance required to be a meaningful part of our world.

I love you,
Audrey

How Do You Communicate?

Dear Mother,

When I took you to the orthopedic doctor today for a consultation about your broken arm, the powerful pain-killing medicine was making you very sleepy—almost totally out of it. I knew that we were in for difficulty when you kept dropping off as we waited for the doctor's arrival. I kept trying to rouse you so that you would be alert enough to respond, but this led only to annoyance on your part and the adamant words, "I'm not sleeping." In my mind, I said, "It's going to be one of those days!" I knew that there were no avenues that would lead to answers from you. I would have to speak for you. At one point the doctor looked at me and asked the key question, "How do you communicate with her?" While I could answer the question by explaining that on good days when your mind was not befogged with drugs we would carry on limited conversation, I realized that he had asked the *real* question: How do you communicate?

I know he just meant how do we talk to each other, but the phrasing of the question led me to ponder, "Do we communicate?" What is it that we do when we get together? Does just being together act as loving communication? Does it need more, and what would be more? Are we communicating because we hear one another, or is this mere socializing? Is there a deeper level that we can reach and be united in our concerns? So many questions come as a result of the one asked by the doctor. In all honesty, I believe we have both lost the ability to communicate. We can answer questions, mention topics of interest, share information about events that occur, even converse about your unreal, delusional world, but somehow over the years of your disabilities we have lost the understanding of how to communicate something of ourselves to each other.

As your disabilities become more pronounced, I ask myself, "How *will* we communicate?" I hope that there is some deep reservoir of feeling carried over from the past that will sustain your memory of communicated love. Perhaps I can find some tactile way to reinforce memories of loving so that we may "communicate" with each other. I want to send out messages of warm acceptance that you are a person who has not been diminished by the aging, disabling facts of your life. I would like to make the doing of this my gift to you for the remainder of your days. It is hard, hard to do this in the vacuum of no response. O God, give me the strength, the love to be a good communicator.

I love you,
Audrey

Non-Communication

Dear Mother,

Today was a whopper of a day. I am sure it was hard for you, even as every day presents its difficulties. This was a day of lost tempers—both yours and mine. When I went to visit you, I couldn't seem to make you hear or catch any of the words I was trying to communicate. You were doing what you so often do—thinking you heard a word or phrase and then making up a sentence to go with it. And then it became even more complicated as I tried to tell you that your thought was not what I was saying at all. We went around and around, with your insisting that

I had said what you thought you heard and my trying to find alternative ways to say the same thing. It was difficult enough trying to get out the sentences that I had started with, without having to try to find ways of telling you to forget what you thought you heard and start it all over again. You ended up by saying, "I'm sure it probably is not important anyway, so let's drop it."

I have such ambivalent feelings about this non-communication. For me, this inability to share even the simplest ideas compounds my sense of frustration, and I find myself wondering why I even try. I know I have been unable to get the basic idea across to you, and now I have to unwind your thought processes before I can even begin again to try for the original statement. Is the message important or vital enough for so much struggle on my part? On your part? I just don't know!

I am aware that it must amplify your feelings of nonworth. I know how you struggle to get one word that will help give you a clue about where the conversation is heading. You have always prided yourself on clarity of thought and rational reasoning power, and now you aren't able to grasp what is being said. It takes so much effort, so much hard work to focus, to try to piece something, anything together. It doesn't work, and you are thrown into total despair.

I left today so frustrated, so angry at you because you were unhearing and so angry at myself that I blamed you for a matter over which you had no control. I was being unloving, and you did nothing to deserve this. Probably the most loving thing I did was to leave and take my anger with me so that another day I could come back and let you know how much I care. Perhaps another day you might hear and comprehend better because all of the annoyance and frustration would not be part of the new day.

I'm sorry today happened, that we were both angry and lost tempers.

I love you,
Audrey

Conversation

Dear Mother,

You have told me over and over again how you wish we could just have fun together—enjoy some interesting conversations with each other—and it is no longer possible. You have shared with me how other mothers and daughters get along and wish that we could enjoy being together in fun times. I have developed feelings of unworthiness because I cannot seem to find any way to make that happen. I know that for you it is just one more indication of your sense of non-worth. How I wish I knew how to make occasions out of my visits with you.

I talk about so many inane things—"Isn't it a pretty day?" "What did you have for lunch (or breakfast)?" I wonder if you don't wish that I would tell you something vital. I know that you, housebound as you are, live through the information that I give you about our lives. But it is so hard to tell you about the exciting things we have done when you only get a word here or there.

I have tried to tell you about what is going on in the world—the war in Bosnia, the presidential election, the fires in California. While you seemed to absorb it, I knew that you could not relate it to anything in your experience, and if I brought it up again, it would be as if you had never heard of it. How could you even recall it, when there is no daily stimulation through newspaper, radio, or TV? Living for you now must be like being in a solitary prison cell, with people only giving you the basic necessities of life. How this affects you, I can only guess—it must be just awful. Your knowledge of this situation must go far beyond that. There is no conversation about this; there are only two people walking separate roads and both feeling lonely.

I realize that it is no longer conversation we share—it is the painful work of trying to find single thoughts to fill up the quiet hours and days that you experience, not only when you are alone, but even when I am visiting you.

I'm sorry that your hearing loss precludes our having deep and loving contacts instead of superficial, unimportant statements.

I love you,
Audrey

In the Silence

Dear Mother,

I just came from visiting you, and today was a day pregnant with silences. I tried to talk with you about the grandchildren, telling you what was going on in their lives, and you did not clearly understand the differences between all of them. So I sat there in silence, pondering in my mind how I could find new ways of saying the same things. I have tried the act of printing out the letters on your arm, and I know now that your sense of touch has disappeared for making out the shape of the letters. Tears well up within me that this means of reaching you is lost.

I don't know what you think in the moments of silence—is it that there is nothing worth saying? In this time I try to think of something to say that you will understand. It is a time when I decide whether the subject I will introduce is worth all the energy it will take to communicate one simple thing. Is my conversational tidbit such that I will end up saying, "Forget it, it's not important"? I know that, for you, everything is important. You want to hear it, to engage yourself in that matter, and when I say it's not important, then I have cut off one more avenue of information.

Sometimes in the silences, I can see through your eyes that your mind is at work, trying to make sense out of the gibberish that has gone through your auditory system. Sometimes it works, and you can come up with the basic thought, and then we are able to move on. Even when we reach this point, I know that we can only talk in simple terms and never have the opportunity to hear the words that your active mind would communicate. What a waste for both of us.

I do know that a nursing home is full of opportunities to be with others—nurses, activities people, staff, and even visitors, but because it is so difficult, you surround yourself with silence. You do not enter into activities because of your disabilities and so you miss out on the moments that would fill up the silent spaces.

There is a profound difference between choosing silence and being infected by silence. I require periods of quiet in which to expose myself to readily perceived stimuli and that which comes in a welling upsurge from within myself. Meditative periods are necessary to my well-being and sanity. I have the privilege of choosing my times of solitude and inner seeking. You have almost all of life with silence imposed upon you like a wet blanket wrapped tightly about you. In the end you can never rid yourself of those suffocating hours, days, and years of silence. How awful, how awful. I'm sorry that I cannot do more.

I love you,
Audrey

Your Own Private Concert

Dear Mother,

It never ceases to amaze me that you hear things that none of the rest of us hear. These sounds are as real to you as if they were going on right in the room. I recall a Thanksgiving dinner with family, when everyone was talking, almost simultaneously. Then you spoke up and told us that the music we were hearing was through the courtesy of the organ at Riverside Church in New York City. You wanted us to be impressed because this music was coming across the miles all the way to Los Angeles. This tidbit was a sound stopper. All of us around the dinner table sat quietly, trying to determine how to respond to this music that was heard only by you. You were enchanted because it came through so clearly. Not knowing how to answer, we gradually resumed the conversations that had been so abruptly stopped, and, little by little, we were back in a pattern that excluded you. You were hearing the beauty and clarity of familiar music. While physically part of the family, eating and basking in the warmth of family togetherness, you were in a world of your own creation that excluded us. How sad that you could not enter into our familial joy and that none of us could experience what, for you, was a time of infinite pleasure. As we resumed our conversation, we laughed at your imaginary music, but we could not laugh at ourselves and our poverty of spirit that kept us from knowing your joy. Mixed connections—over and over again, never making anything but a rudimentary intersection in all our lives.

I recall your decision to create a library of cassette tapes of familiar hymns. You thought, in the earlier days of hearing loss, that you could listen and store up for yourself the words that had influenced your life over all the decades. Favorite hymns were repeated again and again to fill up the void in your life made by lack of conversation. I remember that you gave up joining in the hymns in church many years ago because you were unable to hear the music and tempo. Under your breath you hummed the music; your way of entering into the congregational moments. You attempted to make the words so much a part of you that they would be there when you would need them. You succeeded very well, because on many occasions, you shared with us the names of hymns you heard being sung—and we could hear no songs.

There was the Sunday when we took you to our church, and you commented on how much the service meant to you, since it was all singing. While I had heard a sermon and scripture reading and all the regular parts of the service, your inner ear heard beautiful hymns, and you were blessed. I guess that your lifelong joy in meaningful hymnody had so filled you that you could bring it to the forefront of your mind, thereby making those things you could not see or hear recede, and in its place put you in touch with what was filled with meaning. I am grateful that when there are no satisfying moments, you have this joy unknown to us. What should I do when you tell me about these hymns that are so much a part of your mental process and so absent in my hearing world? You sometimes come up with a phrase from some familiar hymn that only you are hearing and ask me for words or next stanzas. I am at a loss as to how to answer since a fragment with no relationship to anything else is sometimes devoid of meaning. If I pretend that I hear it, I can get all caught up in trying to relate to your memories and I make wrong connections.

Should I deny that the hymns are there? They are real for you and are a blessing. I do not want to deprive you of those uplifting moments, but I just don't know how to let you enjoy those moments when you try to make me part of them. It is a conundrum. I have no solution.

I love you,
Audrey

Noises

Dear Mother,

It seems such an anomaly that when you can't hear common conversation, the daily songs of birds, or the background sounds of everyday living, you can hear noises that we don't hear. You, too, are amazed that we cannot hear those same sounds.

Some of the noises and sounds were the result of your bout with tinnitus—that hearing of a constant, never abating, humming noise that seems to override everything else that is going on—even in your sleeping hours. The continuousness of these noises makes it difficult to get to sleep and even wakes you when you have been fortunate enough to go to sleep.

I can recall your asking me frequently, "What is that noise?" When I responded that there was no special noise, you were positively amazed that I couldn't hear something so loud and so overwhelming of all other sounds. The noise, like squeaky chalk on a board, was so pervasive, so annoying, that it made you almost feel that you would go crazy. It was in everything, surrounding all other sounds, making hearing over it an impossibility, and it was only there for you. How can I understand the feelings that result from such an insidious, terrifying phenomenon? This tinnitus, plus Ménièrre's disease with its accompanying dizziness, plus the nerve deafness, has created such a sense of devastation that I wonder how you have survived it. I know how you worked to overcome the dizziness and kept on as though there were no problems. I am aware of how thoroughly the constant buzzing, loud bangs, and distracting noises affected your whole psyche, and yet you managed to function above this. I suspect that I am one of the few people who was aware of the effort required to keep going.

Even as I admired the ways in which you handled these annoyances, I found humor in your perception that planes were flying over the place where you lived in a constant crisscross pattern in the skies. Not a likely location for a regular flight path. There were so many times that you would look up and say, "The skies have been so busy with planes overhead tonight." With a smile and a rather smug look I tried to tell you that there were no planes flying in that time period. Your answer was always to tell me that there was something about your hearing that picked up on the high decibel sounds and, even though we could not hear the planes, they were there. I do not know at what decibel levels persons with impaired hearing may pick up sounds that those of us with normal hearing cannot sense. It may be that just as dogs hear piercing whistle sounds that we as humans cannot perceive, people like you with tinnitus or nerve deafness have that special quality. I do know that attempting to help you understand that those noises were alien to me was a continuing battle that I lost to you. It really was not terribly important whether or not we agreed with you about the noises, but it was vital to you to have the feeling that you were hearing and doing better than those of us with good auditory function.

The noisiness that made up your days and nights added to the sense of fragmentation that came because of the added distractions. The ambivalence of hearing what others could not was counterbalanced by the fearsome sounds that penetrated only your consciousness, and at times even your unconscious moments, and made life traumatic for you.

I am happy that more recently both the dizziness and the tinnitus seem to be less regular, and the noise has abated.

I love you,
Audrey

LEARNINGS ACQUIRED FROM MOTHER'S DEAFNESS

- The dynamics of relationships between the hearing and nonhearing persons are forever changed. To understand this fact and make adjustments for accommodation becomes the major part of any relationship. It is hard work and takes away much of the spontaneity in pursuing the means of communicating the warmth and love within a relationship.

- Hearing is not a matter only of loudness. It is much more apt to be a matter of discrimination. How to put into a cohesive sentence words that are only partially received, that are confusing because there is no context into which to place them, is a major stumbling block to the hearing-impaired person.

- Communication is more than just spending time with a person. It involves the necessity of relationship. When the normal means of conversing are missing, one needs to consider how to spend quality time that really makes a difference in the life that has become isolated.

- The wonders of equipment for the hard of hearing, surgical procedures, and training are invaluable if they can be utilized in the framework of a person's ability to make use of them. Understanding the demands of all of these validates their usability for the hearing impaired.

• The ability to try to put oneself into the hearing-disabled person's position does not always ensure that there will be a joyous relationship, free of problems. To understand what is going on with the deaf person does not take away the irritation that may be felt by the other person.

• Isolation and silence are devastating to persons who have always been able to be friendly, but who are now impaired by deafness. Silence has its effect on the non-hearing impaired. So much of the time spent with the hard-of-hearing person will be given over to silence and the consideration of how to make meaningful moments of time spent together.

Letters to My Mother Who Is Legally Blind

Like a blind spinner in the sun,
   I tread my days;
I know that all the threads will run
   Appointed ways;
I know each day will brings its task,
And being blind, no more I ask.

I do not know the use or name
   Of that I spin,
I only know that someone came,
   And laid within
My hand the thread, and said, "Since you
Are blind, but one thing you can do."

Sometimes the threads so rough and fast
   And tangled fly,
I know wild storms are sweeping past
   And fear that I
Shall fall; but dare not try to find
A safer place, since I am blind.[13]

The Early Stages

Dear Mother,
   I finished talking with the ophthalmologist today about your cataracts and whether anything should be done

about them. You hoped that the correction of at least one eye might help you to see somewhat better. My conversation with the doctor told me that you would not get the answer you wanted.

I questioned whether your eyesight could be worsened by having this procedure done and learned that it would not create new difficulties, but if the macular degeneration had worsened, there was a good likelihood that there would not be significant improvement in your vision. The question then becomes: Is there any real benefit to be gained from having the surgery, or is it going to make you even more depressed if there is no change? I know that in your desire to be more involved in life any small improvement is worthwhile, but I do not want you to go through the procedure and then feel that life continues to treat you even more unfairly than most people. The decision must be yours, but I recognize that making decisions is not your strongest suit these days. Whenever I talk with you about this matter, you vacillate, and finally each time decide that you will wait a bit longer. I have not pushed you to make a decision. I do not know if you see that fact as another way in which I am failing you. I just know that *you* must decide what to do, and I am equally certain that if your eyesight does not improve you will sink further into a depressive state. Will I, will you be able to handle what that will do to you?

The innumerable appointments with doctors in the early days of macular degeneration were filled with annoyance and very little in the way of positive answers. I remember how catastrophic it was when you found out that most of the eyesight in one eye was gone before you were even aware of the difficulty. Perhaps the later stages of atrophy might have been held off a few years longer, if you had known earlier. We are not certain of how rapidly your vision declined in one eye, but one appointment with a retinal disease specialist told us that there had been so much bleeding in that eye that there was no way they could use the laser technique. An examination of the other eye showed a continuing degenerative track and bleeding so profuse that there was not much hope there either. The retinal specialist, after additional visits, gave us no hope that things would get any better.

I wanted you to accept the doctors' diagnoses as being final and begin to find ways of dealing with this infirmity, but your dogged determination to find ways by almost any means to improve matters made more trips to specialists than seemed necessary to me. I know that you seldom considered the cost of my time. I guess that only the afflicted person can understand the need to keep on trying and trying to find acceptable answers. It must be so much worse when losing the sense of sight eliminates an additional form of communication. Not to see, not to hear really drives a person inward, and then there comes the recognition that there is no means by which to enrich and keep up-to-date the solitary world that will be yours.

You felt bereft. You were bereft. I recognized the end of a period in your life, and then I, too, was bereft. I had lost a mother who had been able to look for the signs of hope in life, who could enter into planning and laughter and being a person worth knowing. Now for both yourself and me, you had assumed the posture of someone constantly in need. You had truly become the child for whom I must take charge—and that made our relationship into something new and untried. I am still working out what this means for us.

I love you,
Audrey

The World of the Unsighted

Dear Mother,

Your macular degeneration has opened up a new world for me. As a sighted person, I have been aware that there are people who cannot see but was terribly unaware of how many people have worked to make it possible for nonsighted people to enter into the sighted world. I learned a whole new terminology; about ways of working around sightlessness; about degrees of blindness and what is involved within the various degrees; about how many institutions address the problem of those who cannot see.

I appreciated so much the time they took at the Braille Institute to figure out what would help you. We looked at magnifying glasses of various intensities and learned that the greater the degree of intensification, the smaller the glass. This means that you can only see a small bit of words, and so reading becomes a tedious, laborious, unrewarding task.

The closed circuit machine that enlarges print so that reading can proceed more easily would also permit you to do such things as sewing, painting, or other tasks that can be done on a flat surface. The options available on this machine are really amazing: light background, dark background; degrees of magnification; lines to make for easier reading. I also learned that there are difficulties to be overcome such as movement from one line to the next, the ability to put together a whole thought when you must constantly be moving the machine to the next word. I learned how hard it was for you in your late seventies to operate the equipment with even minimal efficiency and what tensions that process created for you. Again your determination made you unwilling to give it up when it became apparent that using the machine demanded more of you than you were able to give. Ultimately, this was another defeat for you and sent you into a solitary world more permanently.

Talking books, in the early days before truly severe hearing loss, allowed you to enjoy visits from the outside world by means of those books that stimulated your imagination. Diminishing hearing then made the use of these books impossible because you could not understand the words—and again you lost an outlet that made you believe that you were a real person.

I cannot begin to tell you of the anger/pity on my part as each of these ways around blindness came to a fruitless end. I am sorry that life has hit you with such a double whammy and angry because of what these losses meant about what I would have to do. It is not easy to be the caregiver when you are not always recognized. To come to spend time with you and have you ask, "Do I know you?" followed by the statement "My daughter will be coming very soon and perhaps she can help interpret what you are saying," showed me just how far your eyesight had waned. The frustration of trying to get through to you that I was indeed your daughter was almost more than I could cope with, and my annoyance increased.

I do not care very much for the person I was in those times—annoyed, frustrated, and wishing that I did not have to be there for you. It is really difficult to remember that you do need a loving, caring relationship when you yourself become a nonentity. I translated this into your feelings and knew how much more devastated you were when even the person closest to you was not recognizable.

When I started writing this letter to you, I did not realize that it would cover such a time span and bring back memories better forgotten, but now I see the journey back in time as a means of being aware of how hard you tried to find a way of maintaining your place as a vital person. While I was supportive in taking you places and making sure that the necessary equipment was available for you, I did not understand fully enough all the losses that continued to come to you in exponential form, and I am certain that this lack in me only confirmed your insecurity and fear. Even now, looking back, I do not know what I should have done differently, but I wish I had known then.

I love you,
Audrey

Clocks and Time

Dear Mother,

Time, when you have so much of it on your hands, gets to be burdensome, and it seems as if it will never end.

Out of my own experience, I have learned that there are occasions when time seems to creep by with agonizing slowness. I can be edgy waiting for time to pass. The feelings of unease, slowly moving time, and similar difficulties surfaced as you and I dealt with a variety of situations involving you and time. Clocks, as far as I am concerned, became one of the big nemeses of our relationship. I wish you could understand the history of the various clock, watch, and time sequences.

As your vision problems increased, you had to give up your digital clock because the green lighted numerals were impossible for you to see, and determining the differences between six and five or eight and zero was like perceiving letters in the Cyrillic alphabet. A newly purchased large, round clock that we put up on your wall was no better. You could not distinguish where the hands were. The second hand on these clocks created confusion because at times you thought they were the primary hands, and this threw off your ability to tell the time correctly. We looked at clocks at the Braille Institute, but all of them failed your test of see-ability. Then we purchased a talking clock that gave the hours and minutes, saying, "The time is 2:45 p.m.," or whatever the time was at the moment the button was pressed calling for the time. The problems with this clock were that you could not locate the button you had to press, nor could you understand what was being said. It was a laughing matter for all of us when you indicated that you didn't understand what was meant when the clock said, "Splash forward." It was, however, no laughing matter when we could not convince you that the clock did not say anything like that. You were vehement in your assertion that you had listened to it four times and that was all that it kept repeating. Chalk up another defeat!

The wristwatch episodes were not humorous either. I found a watch that was readable for you, an inexpensive Timex that seemed to meet all your requirements. For a while you were able to see it, but then when I would come to visit you, there was always a new reason for my needing to examine the watch. It had lost two hours or it wasn't going at all—these were only two of the puzzling matters. When I looked at the watch it would be at the correct time. You would assure me that it must have just started again, but how this could be was puzzling from your point of view.

More trips to stores to try to find a clock with black enough hands and large, dark numerals always ended in failure. Your determination again forced me to make unnecessary trips. You don't ever seem to believe that what I, a seeing person, tell you could be true and that your nonseeing perception is inaccurate. I had grave doubts about your ability to make any clock work for you. After one trip, I believe it was three days later that you said, "Well that was another bit of foolishness, because the clock is no good to me." I could have said, "I told you so," but I didn't because I wanted so much to see if there was any way to get around your compulsive need to know the time.

I frequently find you standing at the large wall clock in the nursing home, trying to figure out the time or asking others about it. It is certainly one of the major concerns of your life and so needless, since there are staff people who will see to it that you get to the places where you must be in plenty of time.

Your time, my time, just days and hours have become such an irritation. I never seem able to make things better for you, no matter how hard I try.

I love you,
Audrey

The Use of Time

Dear Mother,

I wonder what there is about time that becomes so important in your world? Does it have to do with keeping control, even when you know that you are not in charge?

43

The concern with time takes up so much of our visiting hours—on my part and yours.

When I tell you when I will next be in to see you, I try not to give an exact time because I know you will be sitting waiting anxiously. Sometimes your internal clock has been wrongly informing you, and almost always you think that I am late or not coming, even though I arrive at just the time I suggested that I would be there. I also know that when I leave I must always tell you the time. I try to relate that time to some activity—a meal, a birthday party held at the nursing home, or some other event. I really try not to add additional stress or worry to your life, and yet there are times that I believe that such stress makes you feel there is a place for you, a need that you can fulfill.

Time hangs heavy for me when I come to visit you. There is so little we can do together, that to fill up an hour requires stamina on my part. I am aware of how often I look at my watch only to find that just a brief minute has dragged by. What can I say to fill the void? I know that nothing I do will take away the feeling that you are lost, because time has no meaning for you now, except hours to be filled with nothing.

We make such poor use of time, and yet I sense that my being there is, if nothing else, a filler-up of stray moments of almost unlimited time for you. I know that when you cease to fret about time, you will have given up all hope. It is my wish that that day not come too soon, but in the meantime, the situation is fraught with tension. I hope that in the midst of all these concerns you will know that in spite of the problems,

I love you,
Audrey

Meals and Eating

Dear Mother,

It just seems that even the most mundane tasks cannot be handled easily. Eating your meals consumes so much energy that for you it becomes unrewarding and further evidence of your lack of control over yet another part of your life. I see the difficulty that you have in trying to get the food to your mouth. You often say that you eat more fork tines than anything else. I have tried to make arrangements for ways to make eating easier for you: a plate with a lip guard that gives you something to push the food up against, thus helping you to keep food on the fork; food cut up into small enough portions to eat. However, there remain those occasions when you are able to eat only tiny, tiny pieces of food. You are concerned because you must remove a piece of food from your mouth and try again to make it into a much smaller size. I know that you feel certain that everyone must be offended by what you deem crude eating behavior. Eating is still one of those skills that you seem able to handle on your own—not nicely, but rather with a bit of mess about your plate. Your reluctance to have anyone help you means that those of us who love you must carefully try to find ways of making certain that there is food on your fork or by turning the plate so that you can see the food with your peripheral vision. I want to make it easy for you to eat, so that you may enjoy the food, but there are times when I am aware that I am playing the "mother hen" too much, and I am sure you wish you could say, "I'd rather do it myself." It really is difficult to know how to help, to know when to relinquish the mother role to allow for that independence that is so essential to you.

I guess, along with the loss of sight and hearing, your taste buds are not as keen as they once were, because you cannot always determine what it is you are eating. The nursing staff tries to take you on a trip around your plate of food, noting items and locations. Entering into the difficulty of doing this are your loss of hearing and your lack of comprehension of what is being said. Nothing is easy or simple any more.

All of these problems could well make you choose not to eat, but you are always there promptly, with a healthy appetite. I heard you say, "The only thing I can do is eat—I serve no other function in company." I appreciate the fact that there is at least one activity that gives you some joy, but how I wish that eating was an experience filled with zest and not just an activity that helps you get through the days of nothingness.

I love you,

Audrey

Clothes, Color, Shapes

Dear Mother,

Well, we were at it again! This time the problem was clothes. Oh, how I hate the seasonal changes. Your unwillingness to let go of the long-sleeved items because we might have a cool day means that I must try to keep enough of the long-sleeved clothes on hand to meet that eventuality. You always seem to doubt that I have done this since you cannot see what I have left in your closet. How I wish I could forget the entire matter.

I think I become the most frustrated when you tell me that your blouses do not go with your pants. A vast array of both long- and short-sleeved blouses in every color combination are kept in your microscopic closet. Since you wear only basic color pants, I don't believe there are any blouses that would not go with almost any you would choose.

The next complaint you offer is that the blouses are so old. While it is true that many of them have been around for a number of years, I guess you forget that I have taken you on trips to purchase new ones on a regular basis. I don't think you even realize which ones are new, since you tell me that everything you own is too old. I have tucked some in drawers for those times when you think you will be left with a short supply; those blouses are never worn because I know you forget they are there.

Then there is your belief that you are totally out of style. Since you cannot see or perceive the style that exists, I do not know what makes you a fashion expert. You are always well dressed, looking fresh and crisp, but no one can seem to make you believe this. I even suggested to some of the staff at the nursing home that they might tell you how nice you look to see if this would overcome your feeling that people were laughing at you because of clothes that are not appropriate. Why do you think that I would allow you to wear clothes that do not look the way I know you want to look? Since I never ask the question, you never give me an answer, and I don't think you could.

Another problem that I have had to deal with over the last few years is taking you shopping. When you tell me that you do not have the right clothes, I have stopped trying to make sense out of that fact, and I take you shopping. One of my worst horror experiences. You think you "see" something that is just what you are looking for, but it isn't the right size. Your arthritis keeps you from being able to wear blouses that go on over the head, and so we must look for button-down-the-front items, and that severely limits our selection. Trying on clothes is one of those terrible moments. I must get you seated, then help remove your clothes, and then put on the new ones. I try very carefully to make certain that they are large enough to go over your hips and protruding stomach, and even when I succeed, you tell me that they are too tight. That isn't so, but to make you believe that the next size is just too big is impossible. This whole matter of clothes being too tight is a problem for which I have no good answers. Your clothes give ample room for movement, but you are insistent that nothing fits you.

Pants are a problem, too. Today I bought you four new pairs of pants that seem to be all right, but in putting them away, you told me that you had too many pants, and I would have to remove some of them. When I try to remove them you will rebel, saying that you need all of them there so that you will have pants that will match your blouses.

If I could have one wish, it would be that the clothing situation, color, style, shape, size, and purchasing, could be farmed out to anyone else who could take these problems, allowing me to forget them. In your working life, you had your own unique ways of assembling your outfits. Why should I think that I could please you?

I don't know how to help you feel good about your clothes. I wish you trusted me. I am frustrated!

I love you,
Audrey

Writing and Correspondence

Dear Mother,

I always thought the word "amanuensis" was a strikingly wonderful term for a person who wrote letters for another; but I never thought that I would fit into that category. You are unable to continue correspondence with your close friends, so I have become your amanuensis. That term doesn't begin to describe the rigors that I go through while attempting to do your letters.

I was truly amazed at how many letters and other loving missives still come to you at your age. I do not have that many people in regular correspondence with me! What an influence you must have been in people's lives to have such a host of people who truly care about you. I am in awe of this!

So many people who write you notes go unanswered until I send out a duplicated letter for you—like your Christmas letter. I know that I can never do justice to your correspondence. Somehow you want me to follow your style of writing, but I know that my efforts do not have the sparkle that is an Ethel trademark. You no longer have any sparkle, so there is no way to make the letters reflect anything but your apathy. While I know that my words are inadequate, I hope they will inform your friends that you still know and care about them.

Writing your letters is such a ponderous time of patiently waiting while you struggle to think of what you want to say. Your long pauses and forgetfulness of where you were in your thought processes make the taking of notes an interminable task—I try to be patient, but it is difficult. Sometimes I want to hurry things along by suggesting ideas that might be put in the letters, but I never strike just the right note and this annoys you. It also slows you down because then we have to go back to recapture your thought processes before we can move on to the next part of the letter.

Occasionally you try to write a letter to a friend. Your writing now is so small and crabbed and all messed in together; the writing is illegible. Not seeing the lines, and not knowing where you began or ended the last word, makes coherent thought impossible. It broke my heart to tell you that no one could read it. Your loss of beautiful penmanship, wittiness, and easily flowing sentences make the tragedy of who you are now a source of new sadness. I know just how much of your self-esteem you have lost. We keep running up against blank walls that lead nowhere.

I love you,
Audrey

Creative Writing

Dear Mother,

The other day I was looking again at a play that you had written that has never been published or performed. It was the last significant piece of writing you did. I remember what it took out of you. You had agonized over your poor typing ability, given your loss of sight, and yet you felt compelled to do this one last drama. Proofreading was needed, since you could not see your typing errors. It demanded much editing because even then the clarity of thought had diminished. After doing my work on the computer, I tried to tell you of the changes that I had made—gave it to you to read. After several weeks of your reading and making changes, I spent more hours at the computer. For you it was a labor of love. For me it was just one more labor to add to an already burdened life.

It will never be printed, since my attempts to find a publisher were unsuccessful because I only tried the easy routes I knew. It would mean the world to you to have it accepted for use since that play would be your final signature on the value of your life. I wish I knew how to make it happen. I have failed.

I love you,
Audrey

On Reading

Dear Mother,

Your avenue to blindness was a slow one, and you felt so blessed during the time that you could read. This ability to read despite increasing macular degeneration amazed the doctors. You wanted so much to be part of the outside world that you became voracious, devouring newspapers, books, and periodicals that would help explain what was happening in your life as well as events in the world. Large-print books and your machine that enlarged the print were in constant use, offering solace as you were able to read and hear all kinds of books.

The Bible was your companion on many days when there was no other outside stimulus, but even that had to go, depriving you of those deep, intimate moments that were valuable to you. Losing the stimulus of reading and recalling those passages of scripture that meant so much to you diminished your ability to bring entire passages to life within yourself. You truly mourned. You begged us to find some way to keep those memory verses intact in your unsighted, unhearing world.

Forgetfulness is not unexpected at your age, but when you cannot refer to the book or passage, then your suffering grows exponentially. It is hard when I cannot be with you constantly to try to assist with the words of the Lord's Prayer or the Twenty-Third Psalm. When you get stuck in the same place time after time, you become frustrated and believe that you have lost contact with the spiritual side of your nature. When I am with you and you forget the words, I can recite these words with you and help in that way, but I recognize that you will forget them again and again.

I have tried reading and rereading certain favorite psalms to you, not as an everyday regimen, but about once a week. The all-important part of that is making sure that you get the words that are so familiar to you so that you can understand the words that follow. I have learned all of your favorite psalms and try to make you aware of those key verses that turn your thoughts inward for inspiration and insight. Your struggle to make sense of the words is reflected in your eyes as you grope for meaning. I sometimes wonder if I am doing you more harm than good by making you struggle so, but since you seem to want me to continue doing it, I have come to the conclusion that even the pain of trying to get the words is better than the awful stillness that gives you no impetus for meaningful thought.

I love you,
Audrey

Reading Your Letters to You

Dear Mother,

Reading letters that come from friends is often a hilarious experience—not that the letters are funny, but trying to find ways of communicating the source of the letter is. I very carefully enunciate the name of the person, and you look at me with that blank stare that says I might as well be speaking Portuguese. I try again, and again I know that I am not getting anywhere. I move on to the next step, which is trying to identify where the person lives or the person's relationship to another well-known friend. Still batting zero. What else can I do? I run through an additional variety of options and decide that they will not help matters, and so I start again with the enunciating of the name. Sometimes it is hopeless, and so I try to tell you what the person has said. This generally does not work, and my patience is worn thin. I suggest that we put it aside and I think, with an even greater degree of warmth, that you accede. Somewhere in our conversation about other things the light begins to dawn and we go back to the author of the letter and can talk about it because some stray fragment has triggered a memory that allows you to finally understand. For me it comes as a great relief that I have been able to tell you of loving friends who want you to know about themselves.

I have a hard time with those friends who feel they must write a dissertation to you. I will have to cut out so much of what is being said, since I can only cover so many topics and must pick and choose the information that is important enough to try to get through to you. A three-page letter can be cut down to about five sentences, for that is all that I can struggle with and all that you can absorb. Increasingly, I have noticed that you don't really care about most of the information. The deaths of your friends or their illnesses are about all that causes you to take serious notice. I suspect that is very typical of persons in their declining years. As I cross out yet another name on your list of friends, I know that one more loss occurs for you, a person who has continued on a downhill road to separation. Again and again I wish that I did not have to be the bearer of intimations of mortality that keep coming to you with such regularity.

I love you,
Audrey

Sight and Negative Reality

Dear Mother,

I cannot tell you how angry, how upset, how hopeless I felt when I left you yesterday. I almost walked out and left you just standing there because I was so distraught. I wasn't proud of myself, so I stayed and managed to calm down, but that sense of dismay stayed with me throughout the day.

There was the matter of your striped blouse—one of those that looks really good on you; it has always seemed to fit you very well. You pulled it out of the closet and said, "Just look at how that shoulder is all ripped out. I cannot possibly wear it ever again. Give it to the rummage sale." I carefully looked it over and could find no place where the seams were unsewn. When I tried to communicate that fact to you, you were incensed that I could not see that the sleeve was hanging down longer on one side. It caused you embarrassment and shame to wear it, and you said you wouldn't. Patiently, I tried to tell you that the blouse was all right. Just as annoyingly persistent was your response, "I know that I am right about this."

I tried to say in as kindly a way as possible, and then not so kindly, that since you could not see, and since I had excellent sight, you should believe my affirmation that the blouse was all right. That was a hopeless argument. I finally resolved the situation by taking the blouse away and telling you that you would not see it again. I guess I wonder why I spent the time trying to make you see the truth of my reality and did not just take the blouse away and forget the whole thing.

My letters to you usually end with the words "I love you," but today I am not sure just how ready I am to say that, so instead I will say,

"I care for you."

Audrey

Newsletter

Dear Mother,

I was so pleased that for all those years when you lived in the retirement community you were able to produce the *Auburn Terrace Times*. It was your lifeline to the real world; because of it you maintained connections with the pulse of your community. The amazing thing about it was that you did it in spite of your visual and hearing handicaps. To be aware of what was happening among the residents was something that required those two senses. It demanded concentration and the ability to focus your attention in a most singleminded way. I salute you for your tenacity, as each passing year made it more difficult to cope with the demands that this monthly paper needed.

Amazing is the word I used in the beginning of this letter, and it truly is the most meaningful word I can employ. Your ability to sit at the typewriter and type all the columns that comprised an eight- to ten-page newsletter, fixing all of the graphics, sometimes even drawing in the items that you wanted, was a phenomenal feat. I recall that you designed the logo for the paper. It was a struggle to make certain that everything came out right. The format and style were equally as important as the content. I know how much this took out of you, since you were dependent only on peripheral sight.

Amazing also applies to the content of the newsletter. That creative mind of yours produced some real winning editorials. Your newsletters always told of upcoming events, introduced new members of the community, shared chatty pieces written by others, and had words from the administrator and from the nursing center. There was never anything too different from what you would find in other house organs, but you added your own flair and style, which made it a warmly human instrument that all who lived in your community were happy to read.

In more recent years there have been so many occasions when joy was not a part of your life that it delights me that I can remember the happy times, even though I know it required almost too much of you. It is important for me to remember times of pleasure when you were able to share these monthly newsletters. As I have been writing these letters to you, I seem to be focusing on those moments that seem to make you less of a person. I rejoiced with you for the significant achievements in spite of handicaps that might have made lesser people simply cave in. The only regret I have is that it is no longer something we can discuss and rejoice in together. I think it might give you some added zest for life when at this time it all seems lost to you. Nevertheless, the joy was there then!

Its toll in time, effort, and thought were tremendous, but it did provide you with something to use your hours, gave you satisfaction, and made you feel like a valued member of your community. I think it was wonderful that you had that opportunity, and I remember well the awful sense of loss that was yours when you realized that you had to give it up. Not only did you lose the time-filler, but you lost the affirmation of your peers—and that was the greater loss. I grieved when that ending created yet another old-age loss. This ending was bittersweet: the joy of having had the experience and the little death that occurred when it was no more.

Life is made up of beginnings and endings, and each of us must make our peace with both. For you, peace has not been easy, but acceptance did take place. For me, I wish that there was some way to ease the loss. I salute you, Mother, for being an extraordinary woman.

I love you,
Audrey

LEARNINGS ACQUIRED FROM MOTHER'S BLINDNESS

- Blindness, like deafness, changes all of life's parameters—for the impaired person and for the caregiver, as well. All the skills and abilities are limited when sight is gone. It is totally pervasive.

- There is a never-ending need and desire to find ways to short-circuit the loss of sight. There are so many options and services available to the unsighted that hours or even days can be spent in seeking new solutions. The caregiver must spend a great deal of time and effort to find those that help and the means of obtaining these services.

- Blindness, even if not total, causes a new understanding about time dimensions, its visibility, and its use.

- Self-perception undergoes drastic changes when one gives up the ability to be responsible for one's own looks. Not being able to see mirror images causes a sense of devastating insecurity. The caregiver is seldom able to be reassuring.

- When a person's life has been filled with joy because of the opportunity to read and write, and this avenue of learning and communication is no more, the unsighted person must find new ways to fill up hours. If having to be reliant on others is a difficult role for the person who has always exercised control, then new problems arise. If the blind person has always been a perfectionist, then sloppy, inexact work will not be acceptable, and so the hours cannot even be filled with "make work."

- The loss of sight, along with other aging disabilities, changes relationships and interactions with friends, families, and, most especially, with the caregiver. Blindness, in and of itself, with no other physical or mental ramifications, can be dealt with on a high plane. Adding other disabilities means major life change and trauma.

Letters to My Mother about Physical Disabilities

This body is my house—it is not I:
Herein I sojourn till, in some far sky,
I lease a fairer dwelling, built to last
Till all the carpentry of time is past.
When from my high place viewing this lone star,
What shall I care where these poor timbers are?

What though the crumbling walls turn dust and loam —
I shall have left them for a larger home!
What though the rafters break, the stanchions rot,
When earth hath dwindled to a glimmering spot!
When thou, clay cottage, fallest, I'll immerse
My long-cramped spirit in the universe.[14]

Looking Down

Dear Mother,

Today was a physically debilitating day for me. I almost had to do contortions in order to be able to look you in the eye. Your increasing disabilities seem to make you stoop over even more, and now you only look down.

Looking down is necessary for your walking, since you have no central vision. You need to pay close attention so that you do not miss things that can be seen with peripheral vision. I never cease to be amazed that you can notice when someone drops something on the floor. You cannot look straight at me, and sometimes you do not even recognize me if the light is wrong, but you can see those little things out of the corner of your eye that others sometimes miss. Having that downward look facilitates your ability to share in even a minimal way with what goes on.

That downward look, however, plays havoc with my ability to communicate with you. Compensating for the difference in our height in order to have eye contact has become more difficult as your stature has shrunk. I could deal with this difference if you would only lift your eyes. Now I must kneel down to be able to look into your eyes. Sitting down is worse, for then you seem to concentrate only on the floor. Trying to get you to hold your head up requires my physically lifting your head. Your puzzlement over why I would do that is hard for me to understand. Even when I am successful at getting your head raised, it is not many minutes before you have eye contact only with the floor. Being able to look into your eyes is sometimes the only way that I can tell if I am reaching you with my words. When you look down, I am lost as to your reactions and must resort to guessing games about what you think and feel. Eye contact does not happen for you any longer, since you cannot see with your central vision, but it creates just one more time that I need to put aside my own requirements and accept what is. It is almost more than I can give.

Eye contact is vital for me to understand what other people are thinking. I know that this will not happen with a person whose head is constantly turned down. I wonder if you have any feelings about this phenomenon or if it is just one more acceptance of disability, or if you are even aware that this is happening. I wish I knew. I wish there was some way to share with you how lost I feel when this means of connection has been severed. I resent the difficulties this physical difference makes for an even fuller relationship. There is no way that you can change. Once again I must accept the situation; I must make the adjustments and move on. Am I able to do it gracefully? I hope so.

> I love you,
> Audrey

Falling

Dear Mother,

Falling is one of those things that you have done many times over the years. When you fell in your younger years your resilience and strong bone structure seem to have made you impervious to breaks. You were most blessed.

In these later years, falls seem to be almost commonplace, but with far greater impact. It started out relatively simply with your losing footing when you had to get up in the middle of the night. You sustained a lot of scrapes and bruises, but no major injury. Your losing balance, however, became such an everyday occurrence that I believed it was unsafe for you to live independently or even in a board and care facility; so we took that step you dreaded most passionately and placed you in a nursing facility. Even in this controlled environment you were prone to many falls—falls that required trips to x-ray or MRI. All nursing homes are required to notify families whenever a patient has a fall. Several early morning calls reported your falls, with information about cuts on your head or the need for the doctor to see you. Even with so many traumatic experiences, you maintained the decisive attitude that you were capable of getting yourself out of bed without the assistance of a nurse, that you were more than capable of walking and tending to your own needs. How shall I proceed to make decisions about what kind of safety precautions should be taken when all my answers will be counter to your perceived abilities? How can I make you see the rationale for making decisions that go against your wishes?

Even as I write this letter, the pattern of falls has increased, and their damage to you has become more pain-filled and more devastating to both your body and your sense of who you are. Your falls have created major trauma in your body and emotional trauma for both of us. I want you safe. You want your independence. We are at an impasse, except that I have the means of control in my hands, and I must choose safety.

I love you,
Audrey

Broken Bones

Dear Mother,

You fell and broke your hip while you were living independently, thus beginning your pattern of injurious falls. You did well in therapy and regained your ability to walk on your own. I was proud of you, your stamina, and the energy you put into making a complete recovery.

The almost regular incidence of falls in more recent times has created major problems. Most of these injuries have been on your right side. The fall when you stubbed your toe and fell over backward caused back problems with referred pain to your right knee and leg. A broken right arm as the result of the next fall created a most disastrous situation. This was only exceeded in pain and difficulty by another fall that caused a broken hip (the same one as before) and a broken right wrist.

I wish I could make you understand that these falls take a toll. Immobilization and assistance for everything that you do, along with wheelchair use and daily therapy are the givens for day-to-day living. At those moments, and for several weeks, you must be totally dependent on the nurses for feeding, dressing, and movement from place to place. I am not sure just how cognizant you are of this, because you keep telling me that you do not intend to be in a wheelchair all the time, that you will remove the immobilizer, that you don't need the restraints of sidebars on the bed or a safety belt on the wheelchair.

I feel bad enough that I am having to make these decisions that I know are against your wishes, but your attitude makes life even more difficult. I just wish that you could trust me enough to know that I only want you safe and to have no more pain inflicted because of another fall or other broken bones.

You are so fortunate to be in a place where every effort is made to give tender loving care. You do not acknowledge this very often because, in your paranoid world you want only to latch onto those things that are not done at the exact moment you want care to occur. I am afraid that your delusions will prevent your understanding of how lucky you are to be in this place.

Your falling is a two-sided coin for me. I care terribly that you have become so prone to falls and hurting, but I also recognize that there is so little I can do to make life better. I teeter on the horns of a dilemma—how can I show I care, and how can I give myself room to resent the inroads of time that I must take because of the effects of the falls? There are no answers. *There are no answers.* I feel defeated. So much of what I have said is about feelings—yours, mine. Are there any absolutes, any real black and white areas and not just this muddied gray? I guess I do not even need to share this with you in your confused, vulnerable state. These feelings are my problem and not yours. Putting them in this letter may just give vent to my need to be valued as a person. I wish we could talk about this.

I love you,
Audrey

Walking and Shuffling

Dear Mother,
Walking was an activity that you always enjoyed. Even when you went into the nursing home, we found many pleasant hours walking together in the out-of-doors. Living in California has allowed this avenue of escape and exercise to be open to you year round. It is hard, though, to talk about your walking, since numerous falls now have made walking a sometime thing.

Age and advancing years have changed your walk. The continuing pain you have experienced as a result of broken bones has made your step more stumbling and inept—created a shuffling gait and caused unsureness in your walking. You still perceive that you walk as rapidly as you once did and that you do it with no difficulty. How I wish that were true. Your perception and the reality are two different things, making this one more area in which I cannot share the truth with you.

Your walking patterns have been interesting. If you have something important on your mind—some errand such as discussing a concern with the nursing home administrator—then you walk more quickly and with great intentionality. When there is a purpose, you shake off some of the lethargy of days filled with no meaning. However, if you just walk, then the shuffling steps take over, the pace is slowed.

After your falls and periods of enforced wheelchair use, after the required therapy to help with ambulation, it became necessary for you to use a walker. I was annoyed that this posed such a problem for you when it gave you greater security. Do you think you are less of a person if you are dependent on things like walkers and are not able to manage on your own?

You are more fearful of being on your own. You seem to know the times when you must be more careful, and while you want to be in charge of your walking, you recognize that you do not have the power, unaided, to move freely. You want a helping hand, but you demand assistance on your own terms, so as not to diminish your being in charge. I have learned to do simple things like counting aloud the number of steps as we approach curbs and stairways. This seems to be acceptable.

Being dependent in such a primary function in life must cause feelings of damaged pride and loss of control of self. In so many ways, you communicate unease and helplessness, showing massive feelings of rejection and annoyance. You are such an independent and assertive lady that you do not accept this state willingly. Walking now is only a regular form of daily exercise, and you are unhappy. I wish you could tell me how to make this seem less threatening to you; how to find more acceptance.

I love you,
Audrey

Wheelchairs

Dear Mother,

Needing a wheelchair after you kept breaking bones was an indignity you did not want to suffer. Your relationship with wheelchairs has been an interesting one.

First, when you lived independently within a retirement community there was resentment. You were unhappy about people coming to the dining room in wheelchairs. They took up a lot of space at the tables and created problems for others. This reflected your first contact with a community in which there were a significant number of disabled persons dependent for mobility on using wheelchairs.

Then, the longer you lived within that community, the more you related to the wheelchair bound. You became the one who frequently went to the nursing part of the facility and took people out for a walk or got them out of their rooms. You were a capable wheelchair walker who wanted others to feel comfortable with their disability. Your first roommate in the nursing facility used a wheelchair. You became her chief "pusher," and I would often find you taking her into some activity, even when your lack of hearing kept you from participating yourself. This willingness to assist others gave you much-needed self-esteem and recognized your need to be a helper.

You went from resentment to acceptance and back again to resentment when you became the one who needed such help yourself. You had numerous complaints about how hard it was to move the wheelchair by yourself, how long it took to get to various places, and other problems related to its use. You resented the security restraints and fought against those things that would keep you from hurting yourself further.

I know you appreciated what the wheelchair could do for you, even though you disliked having to use it. You kept insisting that you would not have that chair all the time, even as I attempted to explain that you had no alternative, since your broken bones seriously upset your balance for walking. I wish that you could think of the wheelchair as a means to get from one place to another, to be a part of the living that goes on in the nursing facility. It is too bad that I can't find the words that would make that wheelchair into a magic carpet, taking you to new adventures, but then, you do not perceive life as a new adventure. I think you are right, there is no magic, there are no adventures, there is just the dailiness of life with someone else taking complete responsibility for your every action. Being wheelchair bound is only one more condition that pronounces your poverty of life. How do you stand it?

I love you,
Audrey

Bladder, Bowels, Bodily Functions

Dear Mother,

I never realized how much of your time and thoughts are concerned with bodily functions. This seems especially true as the years advance. Your childbearing years were responsible for many bladder and kidney infections, causing major problems throughout your lifetime. There were a lot of treatments for these problems and numerous operations for corrective surgery. The toll of all of these physical ailments now shows up in mild incontinence that is devastating to you. Your pride has plummeted because of lack of control. You care little that others are truly incontinent; you do not know about them. Bodily concerns become totally self-absorbing because there is so little else to occupy your mind. I am saddened by this and know there is nothing I can do. Your bowels take up hours of our conversation. How I wish there were other conversations that we could have. How I wish that you did not think that there was something I ought to do about the problem. I really don't know which is worse: looseness or constipation. At this moment constipation is the culprit. I hold regular conversations with the doctor about your concerns. I hold regular conversations with the staff of the nursing home about this situation. We have worked out medications, prunes, specialized bulk-producing diets, laxatives, suppositories, and heaven only knows what else, and I still fail in your eyes.

You believe that you have some kind of growth that no one takes seriously. We have been the route of colonoscopies and upper and lower GI series. The doctor says that the elasticity and muscle control is gone and that there really is little that can be done except to keep on with all those items noted above. You really rebel at this course of action and somehow expect us to do more—and there is no more to do.

You want all of us—doctor, nurses, me, to listen to the infinite detailing of the problems relating to your bowel functions. They are so important to you. If I do not listen and relate to the discussion of your ailments as if it is of world-shattering importance, then I am not taking the matter seriously. The doctor, too, has become persona non grata because what he does is not adequate in your tortured mind. I am sorry that we make you feel that we are indifferent. While it is terribly important for you, I know that we are all trying to do the best we possibly can. You and I are at an impasse that cannot possibly be resolved. You feel powerless, and I am merely frustrated that there is so little acceptance of life's reality.

I love you,
Audrey

Medications

Dear Mother,

Medications have always been a problem, especially those that have not worked well for you or caused side effects. You usually required the strongest possible medicine before the "bug" or virus could be conquered. You have had enough problems so that when diagnosed you could tell the doctors what medicines would work.

When you were sure you had a bladder infection, I talked with the nursing staff, saying, "She has had enough of these infections that she usually knows what her problem is. I believe you should take it most seriously." You were right and the antibiotic prescription from the doctor cleared it up very soon.

The medication given for your delusions was a strong antidepressant drug. The large doses required to bring calm to you turned you into a zombie; certainly not an alert human being. The doctors tried to achieve balance by cutting down on the dosage and yet making certain that you had enough to take away the terror and fears that were part of your delusions and paranoia. Unfortunately, while we didn't succeed in removing the fears, you seem to have fewer visions of persons needing your help for their lostness. I am so grateful that the doctor is willing to constantly evaluate the dosage to keep you on an even keel. The last thing I want is for you to lose all sense of the world around you because you are overmedicated, even though I know that we take a chance of increasing your paranoia.

Your refusal to ask the nurses for simple pain relievers when you need them is really difficult to understand. Your paranoia and your inner fantasy life certainly cause enough mental anguish, so, at this point in your life, I can see no reason for you to be uncomfortable and in physical pain. You believe that the nurses will not give you the help needed unless I ask for it. I sometimes want to shout at you or shake you because of your refusal to try to do anything for yourself that makes life easier and takes away the pain.

I am not even sure why I wrote this letter to you because it does not have any answers. It simply recounts difficulties. Even if you could read this letter, would it seem believable or help you to find important insights into yourself? I think not, so I will just end this letter by letting you know that

I love you,
Audrey

Hair and Skin

Dear Mother,

Today I can rejoice that you can accept your looks and how you appear to other people. You have had that kind of youthful face that did not seem to show wrinkles or what the aging process was doing to you. You are so fortunate that the lovely look of a person who has lived life joyously has carried over into your senior years. I marvel that you never seem to question much about your looks.

While you are aware that you have dry skin, I am the one concerned about it. I want to keep it lubricated and soft so that your looks will last your lifetime. Caressing you with lotion not only helps to do this, but is one of the tactile ways in which I try to communicate my loving concern. I hope that as I age I may have skin as clear and unmarked by the testings of time. I thank God that, though you have other problems, your appearance can give you a sense of happiness.

On the other hand, today was another day of adamant denial of the truth of reality. Hair is today's problem: hair so fine that it has difficulty holding a curl and, at this time, so thin that it barely covers your scalp. It is utterly impossible to please you, since you think your hair should look as if you came from the hairdresser on a daily basis.

We never seem to be working on the same track at the same time. Yesterday I told you that it was time for a new permanent, but you said, in no uncertain terms, that you would not need one for several more weeks. Without the permanent all the curl will be gone by Tuesday, and you will be unhappy. I lose again, and you become even more agitated.

The hairdresser tries so hard to please you, but I hear only disparaging remarks. I know these remarks are only made to me so that I will do something about your perceived problem. It is difficult enough dealing with those matters that have a basis in reality, but when I have to grapple with your perceptions about your hair, when I cannot convince you that everything is all right and you look great, then I am truly stymied. How can I deal with the shadows and mirrors of your interior thought processes that bear no relationship to the world of reality? To agree with your ideas of how your hair looks would only cause unhappiness. A vicious circle has been created with no way to put an end to the process. It is hard for me to deal with your negativism when there is little hope for any positive improvement. Unhappiness is the key word here—both yours and mine. Is there any pathway that will lead to joyful acceptance?

I love you,
Audrey

Teeth

Dear Mother,

You are so fortunate to have reached your age and still have your own teeth. Your confusion about your teeth, however, makes one more problem for me. Regularly you tell me that you need to get to the dentist because of cavities and holes in your teeth, and regularly I take you to the dentist, and regularly the dentist says that your teeth have no cavities, and regularly you do not believe him.

Your perceptions are so off center that the information you give me about what is happening to your teeth becomes almost ludicrous. I do not know what you mean when you tell me that the teeth have rubbed together in such a way that food gets down into the gum and creates major cavities. Your fear that you will have to deal with false teeth is not even in the realm of possibility at this late stage in life. I know I can't say anything that will be believable to you, and so periodically we go through this same routine.

X-rays have been taken, regular cleanings and check-ups done and you will not be convinced that this is as good as it will get. You cannot see your teeth, and I will not tell you that the holes between your teeth are caused by your advancing age and a certain amount of shrinkage of the gums. When I look at your teeth each tooth seems to stand alone. They are very thin, almost opalescent, like mother of pearl, and no amount of cleaning seems to be able to dissipate the yellowish cast. I am sure that they no longer feel like the teeth you have known through most of your life. I want you to have as good feelings as possible about how you look. I want us together to find a way to rejoice that you have your own teeth and that they continue to serve you, if not well, then at least adequately.

All the physical losses, one on top of the other, must be so disheartening, so disillusioning. As you sit there in your silent world do you reflect on the parts that are disintegrating, those things over which you have no control? So much of what you require from me has to do with complaints about your physical presence. All the changes you experience cause me to contemplate what that will mean for me as I age. Will I grow old any more gracefully or perhaps not as well? I do not have a clue about how I will react if such a fate is mine.

It's peculiar that, even as I write these letters to you, I reflect on the ramifications for myself. I realize that I cannot make things better for you, but maybe, just maybe, by pondering my own feelings I can stop internalizing my failures with you. Wouldn't that be wonderful!

I love you,
Audrey

LEARNINGS AQUIRED FROM MOTHER'S PHYSICAL DISABILITIES

- In the later years of life, increasing physical disabilities become an accepted pattern for many.

- Fear relating to all kinds of ailments takes over conversation. Concern for the body and bodily functions is frequently the major concern of the person whose life has become constricted by time and place. A rational approach to irrational concerns about bodily ailments is seldom understood by an aging parent.

- Safety and continuing care become paramount issues for the caregiver of an elderly parent. Frequently, even when this is not the choice of the caregiver, a nursing home becomes the only viable choice.

- Lack of mobility places onerous burdens on the caregiver when the aging parent still wants to believe that he/she is capable of doing most of the tasks of younger years. Trying to physically move persons around demands learning new skills for handling impaired persons.

- The lack of willingness to understand how debilitating bodily changes can be places both the aging parent and the caregiver at cross-purposes and so changes the dynamics between these persons in significant ways.

Letters to My Mother about Dementia/Hallucinatory Affects

Bowed by the weight of centuries he leans
Upon his hoe and gazes on the ground,
The emptiness of ages in his face,
And on his back the burden of the world.
Who made him dead to rapture and despair,
A thing that grieves not and that never hopes,
Stolid and stunned, a brother to the ox?
Who loosened and let down this brutal jaw?
Whose was the hand that slanted back this brow?
Whose breath blew out the light within this brain?

O masters, lords and rulers in all lands,
Is this the handiwork you give to God,
This monstrous thing distorted and soul-quencht?
How will you ever straighten up this shape;
Touch it again with immortality;
Give back the upward looking and the light;
Rebuild in it the music and the dream;
Make right the immemorial infamies,
Perfidious wrongs, immedicable woes?[15]

I guess I wasn't alert enough to recognize all the symptoms that led to the dementia. I listened to the stories and realized that they were hallucinations, but did not fully recognize in the early days how many of my mother's

71

waking moments were consumed with these inner visions. Wrapped up in all these delusions was the need to be of help to people—either individuals or in a group. The cast of characters changed over a period of time, but not the need to be helpful. Most of the delusions seemed to be caught up with family, my mother's own fears, and a mixture of well-known personalities. A psychologist might be able to separate the various fragments, but for me it really made no difference because I was, and continue to be, caught in the middle of concepts and ideas that do not yield to logical conclusions.

In the beginning the hallucinations involved children—sometimes grandchildren, now all married adults, and their need for someone to help them get to various places. Mother perceived them as dreams, but scary dreams, that kept her awake at night. As the dementia increased the children were no longer family, but a boy who was being abused and then one who climbed up onto high places. Mother was always seeking to find the means by which she could rescue this child.

The hallucinations became really frightening when they were life threatening—riots that were going on within the place where she lived. A boy-child was caught amid these riots, and mother had to try to save him. In one of these problem times at 3:00 a. m. she knocked on neighbors' doors trying to find a way to get to him. She called 911 three times in one night. My frantic mother called me at 6:00 a. m. asking me to come—and come I did. I was not able to dispel her fear or convince her that this was a hallucination. I did bring her back to my home and talked with the psychiatrist with whom we had already made contact.

A brief stay in the mental health wing of a hospital brought about some calmness and gave us the verdict that there was no physical reason for this behavior. We came to recognize that the sensory deprivation had caused her to develop hallucinations. Other than giving her medication to control the fearful, threatening aspects of her hallucinations, there was no answer.

Today we try to maintain a balance so that the drugs do not make her into a zombie and yet control the worst of the hallucinatory fears. I am not certain that we succeed too well because I sense that the hallucinations are winning out.

The hallucinations took on a totally different appearance, and, in the middle of the loneliness and solitariness, Sandy came into my mother's life. Sandy was a woman who had a lovely solo voice, and she sang songs to Mother. This singing was heard from wherever Sandy was in concert throughout the country. It came to Mother through some mysterious network that allowed her to be plugged into these restorative periods that gave her solace. I was never able to be part of this network, much to my mother's chagrin.

Sandy was no ordinary person, for she was well along in life. At one time I asked how old Sandy was and was told that she was 149, but she told people she was 87 (mother's age at that time). Sandy was continually in trouble. She had had miscarriages, an abortion, cancer surgery, throat surgery, and mental breakdowns. Sandy was evidently also somewhat of a femme fatale, for she attracted men to her. Her husband had to be put in an "insane asylum," and Sandy did not know how she would pay for it. The saga of the various places Sandy had lived covered everywhere from New England to California and even some place on the "Canadian border of Massachusetts." While living in Georgia she would then appear at a hospital in Boston, Massachusetts. It was very difficult to keep up with her movements.

At some point Sandy changed her name to Lottie— but she was the same person. Lottie was a great comfort to Mother, but also a cause of great concern because she was forever being evicted from homes and lodgings. Lottie was continually caught up with singing groups who were very loud and boisterous and made life difficult for those around her.

Still later on, Sandy/Lottie was to become known as Frances. The latest name change was Marian. I never knew of any reason for these changes in name, but not in person. The peccadilloes in which she was involved were not affected by the different nomenclature. Frances frequently had all her clothes stolen, money stolen, men who married and divorced her, and continual evictions from many abodes. She spent a great deal of time in police stations following her evictions from various homes. Riots frequently occurred, and Frances somehow seemed always to be caught in the middle of these altercations.

What happened to Sandy/Lottie/Frances/Marian was always critical and always demanded that I do something to alleviate the situation. There has been no way in which I could counteract these frightening dilemmas.

Now in present times, in addition to the Marian stories, there is the hallucination of persecution by the nursing home in which she lives. There is a constant fear of being forced out of the home, of nasty and slurring remarks made about her, and my lack of understanding of her reality. My mother is terribly confused, living as she does between the real world that includes family and nursing home and the unreality of her hallucinations.

Friends and Visitors

Dear Mother,

What a terrific testimony to your life! Imagine, you still have friends who come to see you on a regular basis, even with all your disabilities. Some of my friends make the effort to seek you out, so that there is a regular cadre of people who take time to chat with you. You are so blessed, and you do not even recognize it.

What I have observed lately is that you shut yourself down, shut yourself off, and never really enjoy the visits. You think you have nothing to share with anyone since you do nothing. You are afraid to take a chance on an activity that might prove beneficial, since you may not do it well. That's understandable, but it robs you of having something to share with others. I wish that you would try, even with the risk of failure, but you won't.

It saddens me to hear you say that it would be better if some of your close friends would stop coming to see you. When a faithful friend comes to see you weekly, bringing news of your church, you believe that you have nothing to offer her. I think that the fact that you have been good friends is valid enough reason for both of you to enjoy visits. I know it must be difficult to engage in conversation when you do not hear and have no current areas of shared living. I am sure that there appears to be no benefit for either of you when she must do most of the talking. What happens in this situation reminds me of some words from *Living with the Disabled*:

> Disability can destroy a friendship. Often a disabled person can no longer participate in the shared activities that bind friendships together.[16]

This is what is happening, and it is sad.

Hiding out way back in your room, away from the bustle, the comings and goings, and the activities that are offered is a one-way street to having even less to offer to friends and visitors. Since you are hidden away in the back, it isn't easy to be friendly, even for those who seek you out—chaplains, your pastor, and one or two others.

Your inability to see people makes quick identification impossible, your hearing loss makes getting their names more of an adventure than you want to try, and all of the visit becomes a chore. I imagine you must think, "Is it worth it, is it worth straining myself when I shall not succeed?" If I could give an answer, I would have to say, "What have you got to lose by trying?" Sharing with a friend who is willing to be there for you is almost certainly better than sitting in isolation. I realize, though, that that is my perception. It is not yours. You seem to have almost given up. What will you do with the rest of your life if you choose to close off these friendly visits?

Wanting to motivate you to find new channels for friendship is not enough; finding significant answers is not enough. *You* have to want to do this job, and you don't desire it enough. You are choosing your own road, and it diverges from mine. Which one is the way to go?

Companionship is food and drink for the human spirit. All people, in all cultures, in all of recorded history, have sought the pleasures of companionship and suffered when it was lacking.[17]

I think you are suffering from lack of companionship—other than mine, of course, and suffering is not what I want for you. How do you find companionship in a sightless, silent world? I have no good response to that question. I only know it saddens me and creates horrendous loneliness for you. Another quandary that leads only to dead ends.

I love you,
Audrey

Fear of Being Alone

Dear Mother,

I hated to tell you that I was going to be away for a week or ten days. I waited almost to the last possible moment so that you would not have time to mull it over and think of all the reasons why I should not go. I know that it is a fearsome time for you since I am your security blanket. If there was some way in which you could, like Linus and his blanket in the *Peanuts* comic strip, drag me around, I know you would.

You immediately begin to worry about having money to do things, that no one will be able to reach me, that no one else can take care of items that come up, what will happen with your hearing aid batteries, and the list could go on and on. I am aware that these are just the outward manifestations of your inner terror that you will be forsaken. Even when I make arrangements for others to be there, you are still fearful.

Your dementia seems to take over much more completely, and you are frequently frenzied to such a degree that others are most fearful for you as well. Your hallucinations take on more terrifying shapes and concerns. You have delusions that I have come back and then not spent time with you. Your entire health seems to go on a downward curve. You worry that I will not be there to work through these problems.

Even being in a care facility where everything is done for you does not give you surcease from your fears. You will be nursed and cared for and even visited, but you will still feel anxiety. I know of no way that I can help alleviate these feelings of distress, short of never going anywhere. I do not know how to help you find serenity even at the times I am with you; my frustration at finding solutions to the insoluble problems that terrorize you is even greater when I am to be away.

I struggle with what my being away should mean to me. I have become comfortable knowing that there is no need for concern medically. I am certain that it is terribly unwise and selfish for me to think that you should be able to live with this kind of fear even for short periods of time. Equally certain is the fact that for my sanity I must live my own life. I want to continue to try to find ways of bringing solace to you in these circumstances. I wish it could be different.

I love you,
Audrey

Loss of Memory

Dear Mother,

You really are no different from lots of other people in their eighties who have suffered significant memory loss as they have aged. However, I find it interesting how often you cannot remember the name of your imaginary friend. You call her "what's-her-name" but, unfortunately, do not go blank about her problems. How I wish you would forget the problems and just remember her name.

The more disturbing memory loss to you seems to be with long-term memorized passages of scripture. The Twenty-Third Psalm, which you try to say as a means of solace for yourself, is forgotten, and you get hung up on "Yea though I walk through the valley of the shadow of death." When I say it for you, you go along very well until we reach that point and then once we have overcome that lapse, you can continue on. You tell me that saying it with me is helpful, but when you are alone and try to recite these words, then memory loss takes over. I don't know how to help you so that you may find peace and hope from this passage.

There seems to be something about the Lord's Prayer—"give us this day our daily bread" that won't come to mind. No matter how many times I tell you the words this phrase seems to be the sticking point.

I recognize that the problem of memory loss is only symptomatic of a spiritual decline and a deepened sense of loss. Your faith does not seem to be able to overcome what happens when memory goes. When you can't see and can't hear, then stored-up remembrances of meaningful words of wisdom, passages of poetry, the words of hymns, and fragments of thought that suddenly evaporate from the memory become still a further burden for you to bear. It is as if somehow one more piece of yourself is missing. How many more pieces can be taken away, without something to replace the inspiration and sense of wholeness that you had?

It is difficult to comprehend how these memorized passages that come out of your past can be lost over and over again, and yet if you are asked about long-term memory, you can regale us with information and pertinent facts. What stirs up the dates and times of events that occurred over the span of years, but keeps dormant those words that allow you to keep pathways to inspiration closed? There is no longer any possibility that you can learn poetry or hymns, there is no way that rote repetition can be given to you. There just seems to be a continuing stream of lost opportunities leading to hopelessness. Life is not meant to be this way. I am at a loss to know how to bring back either memory or hope.

I love you,
Audrey

Imaginary Friends, Imaginary Needs

Dear Mother,

Your urgent call to me yesterday had to do with Frances, your imaginary friend who fills up your lonely hours in ways unknown to me. So many of the problems you encounter in life at this period come out of your dementia/hallucinations. Today's problem, told to me in vivid, lengthy detail, was a call for help from the doctor who was with Frances. In this episode she was in a hospital receiving treatment because some ruffians had hurt her. At the time of her release, the doctor told her that someone very sensitive and careful would have to care for her. None of the nurses would do the job in the right way. The doctor talked about others who might help, but since Frances is totally without friends, the doctor asked if you could go with her to see that she got safely to her home. You told me that Frances was sure that you would not be allowed to do it, but asked anyway.

Mother, you were trying to get my approval to be her companion, but I had a lot of questions: How would you get there? Where would she be going? How would you get back? You assured me that the doctor knew where you were to go and would take you and bring you back. There was to be an overnight, but you would not even need to pack. You saw it as a kind of fun trip that you would enjoy.

My response that I did not see any way that it would be possible was most deflating, and you kept referring to the subject over and over again. Your desire to be a helper just keeps recurring again and again, and I keep on being the one who must say no. It would be easier just to go along, but I know that saying yes would have its ramifications: You would pack, get dressed to go, and then sit and wait and wait and wait. No one would be able to convince you that the doctor wasn't coming for you. Closely monitoring those unreal ideas with what will happen if I agree to them forces me to wish for some easy answers to your misperceptions. I keep hoping that I can find some consistent way of dealing with each situation as it arises, but there is none. I must fly by the seat of my pants time after time.

I alerted the nursing staff to your concerns in case you still might attempt to go to the aid of your friend. Since no call came from them, I assume you resolved this dilemma within your own demented reality. I hope it was not too painful. I hope you think that I cared about you and your friend. I wish, I wish, I wish, but it doesn't seem to do much good.

I love you,
Audrey

On Making the Unreal Real

Dear Mother,

Today only proved that my poor attempt to make your unreality real is a losing cause. While I came away laughing, I was further frustrated by how little I am valued.

I remember that you begged me to write a letter regarding Frances to the person who acts as her conservator. You had a name and address—such a city never existed—and I was to tell Mrs. Johnson that Frances had no money and needed help because she needed surgery. I suffered patiently through your struggle to tell me what needed to be said, even writing it all down. While I told you that I had done the letter and mailed it off, that was an untruth. You kept waiting for a response because Frances was in such desperate need. You asked me to write another letter and gave me a different address.

Not knowing how to deal with this traumatic situation that was taking up all of your thought processes, making you very nervous, and feeling lost because you were unable to do something, I made up a letter of response. I shared with you that Mrs. Johnson had sent a letter, apologizing for not having written before. According to my made-up letter, Mrs. Johnson had moved to the state of Washington and so had not responded. However, now that she was settled she had made arrangements for Frances to go into a retirement community known as "Happy Home." This was a wonderful place not too far from her home, and she would see to it that Frances had clothes and meals and would take care of her for the rest of her life. Mrs. Johnson would supervise her finances and be able to see her regularly.

Mrs. Johnson was to come to California, fly back with Frances to Seattle, and get her settled into this home. You were so relieved that "you had done something right" and happy that Frances would be cared for so well.

Unfortunately, I went out of town for several days during the time while this transfer was supposed to have taken place. Upon my return you told me that there had been some trouble, and they had not left on the day they should have but were going on the day I returned. Just a few days later you informed me that there had not been a very thorough investigation of the retirement community. It was run by a very conservative religious group of Anabaptists, and Frances did not meet their standards, so she had been evicted from the premises.

I know now that you cannot make the unreal real, because your reality is always better than mine. You took my made-up retirement community and imbued it with a strange reality that made it unacceptable. I wanted to laugh at what had happened. I decided that I would not try to play your game ever again, because I would only lose out to your delusions.

It is so odd, Mother, to be in this position. I know that if you could be aware of your delusional behavior, you would just cringe and apologize for what you put all of us through. I know that my poor attempts at permitting you to be the helper just backfire, and you come away unsatisfied with what I do. I know there is no answer, and so I am learning to laugh at the ridiculousness of these forays into unreality. I guess it is better to laugh and put aside these fantasies than it is to cry over what has happened to change you from a creative, intelligent woman into this woman who seeks to make her world into a place where she has value. Even when I try my best, I so seldom meet your high standards of the way to help others—and in your eyes I am diminished in your unreality. I am sorry that I am such an ineffective instrument, but saddened that you have so little belief in my efforts.

I love you,
Audrey

Thoughts about Negative Reality

Dear Mother,

Just recently I wrote you a letter about negative reality. I have better formulated my thoughts on this matter. I keep being amazed at your unwillingness to believe almost anything I tell you. I know there is no rationality to your perceptions, and yet it is a constant source of irritation that my ability to see and your nonrecognition of what I tell you as truth is not only doubted, but labeled as incorrect information. Sometimes I wonder if I am the one with major problems.

Have I really been reduced to always making your unreality the only reality there is? As I have read books on senior aging and lack of reality, I have discovered that you just fit into the category of those for whom your unreal world is more believable than the reality we cognitive people know and experience. I find this difficult to live with, and yet that seems to be the only route for my sanity and for keeping my own mental health in balance.

Your lack of sightedness, together with your hallucinations and loss of grasp of reality takes a real toll on me. It causes situations like that which happened yesterday. It really is not worth stirring up both of us, and I must take responsibility because of my inability to just let matters go on as you perceive them—but it is hard.

I remember reading the following "Caregivers' Bill of Rights" in the book *Elder Care*, by James Kenny:

> You must survive, and you have that right.
>
> Sometimes you need a few hours away from your elderly parent. You have the right to go off and find yourself again in some personal pursuit.
>
> You have the right to get help. You are not indispensable—others can act in your place.
>
> You have the right to be patient with yourself and your own limitations. It is one thing to be patient with your aging parent; it is even more important to be patient with yourself.[18]

These words continue to resonate with me after a day like yesterday. How much good am I doing if I cannot accept my own limitations? Am I assisting you? I don't know. I guess I can only do my best and recognize that my humanity, my need for affirmation, is important too. Today I can say,

I love you,

Audrey

Paranoia

Dear Mother,

I know that delusions, hallucinations, and paranoia are all mixed up together in your inner world. The hallucinations feed your paranoia, and then your paranoia informs your delusions of unreality. You seem to have two kinds of paranoia going currently, and sometimes they even interact. I am sure that they grow out of your fears about your status in life over which you have no control of events, but rather are controlled by your physical limitations.

It is impossible to deal with your paranoia about your noncommunicative roommates keeping you awake at night talking about you, putting you on the carpet for things you have or haven't done. You tell me how they talk about your clothes, about what you eat and how you eat, about how they want you to get out of the nursing home because you create trouble. It almost seems to be a courtroom in which you are not given a chance to defend yourself.

The other fear that seems to surface in your paranoia is that you are actually being forced out of the nursing home. The administrator is the culprit in this situation. These eviction notices always seem to occur at night when the administrator is not there, but the hallucinations are so strong that you don't believe my word.

I find myself being embarrassed by having to ask the director of nurses or the administrator to confirm that you will not be evicted. Both of them have been so helpful, kind, and gracious, spending time trying to calm your irrational fears. Even if it works temporarily, we come back again and again to this same scenario.

I appreciated the administrator's taking the time to write you a letter saying that you would be in the nursing home as long as you needed the services. I read you the letter and then put it in your Bible on the dresser so that whenever you had another visitation about being evicted you could show the letter. Two days later you informed me that "they" knew about the letter and that it had no value. This time when I contradicted you and said that "they" were wrong, you more or less believed me. You said, "Well, we'll just have to wait and see." I sense that your fears have not really been diminished, but that they are in abeyance for the time being instead. What more can I do to give you the necessary feeling of security when your fears are so great? Logic does not seem to be a useful tool, nor does my attempt to move into your unreality. I guess there is no real answer, but I want so much to help you feel safe. When I think about the "needs" we all have for our lives, I am reminded again that we are talking about basic, primal needs and not something higher on the scale.

You and I have always dealt with life on a much higher plane, and I am finding it disconcerting that now there are only these basic concerns. Turning your creativity into delusional behavior at the most primitive level seems to have diminished both of us. I hope that if I have this same problem I can retain enough of my own sense of worth that I may be secure. How wonderful it would be if I could break down the dividing wall of paranoia that separates us. It looks pretty dismal to me. It must seem most fearful to you.

I love you,
Audrey

Lack of Trust and Belief

Dear Mother,

I am really getting so tired of not being believed. There is no way to get through to you with truth when your delusions take over. You are always so certain of your facts that even when I tell you that events did not occur you cannot believe me.

Your recurring hallucinations about riots going on in the places where you live are frightening for you and cause you great distress. If you could just accept my words, they might bring you some surcease from the anguish you go through.

How many days have you asked me these questions, "Did you get home all right after the trouble last night?" "What time did you finally get home?" Your understanding about the rioting takes different forms. Sometimes it has to do with Frances and me, sometimes with riots going on with striking nursing staff. These events seem to happen between 9:00 p.m. and 2:00 a.m.

I was distressed the time you told me that Frances/ Marian, the imaginary friend, and I got into a major fight, and that I had cut her severely enough for her to go to the hospital. I had also been hurt with a slash on my face, but that was not as serious as Frances' injuries. Your information that the doctor had brought me home from the hospital bore no resemblance to reality. I could not seem to make you believe that I had been to the movies and was not even near your nursing home. I repeated numerous times that I had not been there and that I had not been hurt. I tried to convince you that it was all a hallucination. It was, however, so real to you that not even feeling my smooth, uncut face helped. I tried valiantly to explain to you that I never physically fight with people and so could not have hurt Frances/Marian. I asked you to try to remember when I had ever hurt people in that way and you admitted that I have never been physically hurtful to anyone, and that I had never lied. Still you found it impossible to believe that this event had not occurred.

I wonder why your mind conjures up so much violence. I wonder why you think of me in such unflattering terms. Over the years, as two adults, I have always thought our relationship was warm and caring, full of interesting talks, and filled with great respect for each other as human beings. I know that you are confused, but what has changed me from being a worthwhile person into someone more closely allied to an ogre? In your rational, lucid moments you see me as I really am, but how much I dislike your emphasis on a perceived unkind, uncaring side. I know that I have never been this awful person. Where does it come from?

This lack of trust, this lack of belief takes its toll on me. Hearing on an almost daily basis of my selfishness, my unwillingness to help, my physical harming of people makes me angry at first and then terribly, terribly saddened to think that I have degenerated so far in your estimation. I ought to be able to say it really doesn't matter because these are hallucinations and delusions, but the everyday repetition calls into question my own feelings about myself. I know this shouldn't be so when I know that this is not who I am, but it is like a canker that eats away at me. Maybe, if just once you could commit yourself to believing in me, I could forget all the other times. I recognize that I am expecting from you something that in your state of dementia it is not possible for you to give, but I want you to know that having you trust and believe in me would bring great joy. Bringing great joy to me is not high on your agenda, which is so fraught with your own basic needs. What a dilemma for both of us.

Nevertheless, I love you,
Audrey

Sins and the Need for Forgiveness

Dear Mother,

You have been so overwrought, so concerned about your "immortal soul." You have kept seeking out people who will listen to you confess your wrongs, listen to the evil that you say you have done. You continue to seek absolution. I have tried to reassure you that God's love and forgiveness reach all of us. I cannot imagine any "sin" that you might have committed to cause you so much distress, cause you to worry about what will happen to you after death. I realize that my words do nothing to assuage the guilt that you characterize as a large lump in the pit of your stomach. I have no magic wand that I can wave over you to help you with this trauma.

I know how real it is for you. The appointment with the pastor of your church really did no good. I even wonder if you told him about the "sin." Obviously he had no balm for your soul. At the nursing home you spent a lot of time with the chaplain, and your report was that she was the most helpful person so far—but she still did not alleviate your fear.

I cannot believe that a "sin" that occurred, as you tell me, in your childhood can at this time in your life assume such vast proportions as to make you fearful of what will happen to you in eternity. The entire matter is so difficult for me to understand because throughout your life you have been caring and helped others. You have been there for people through times of trauma. Your deep belief in a meaningful prayer life and your understanding about a loving God have been central to your identity. What has happened to you in these later, senior years that has undermined your trust in a God of forgiveness?

It seems to me that you are looking for *judgment*. Do you really want to be struck down for something that happened in your childhood? What visible symbol that you would accept could be given that God has forgiven you? Contrary to your belief that I do not take this matter seriously, I have spent much time pondering some way in which to give you some inner peace. I realize now that no matter what my words, the only satisfying solution is one that you will propose. That puts us between a rock and a hard place, because at this point in your life you are incapable of making a decision.

How can a rational person create a framework for acceptance for a person whose inner thinking processes and ability to delineate between real problems and hallucinatory ones is skewed to unreality? I have given up discussing this matter unless you bring it up and hope that I may yet find a way to convince you that God still loves you.

I recognize that when there are no other matters with which to concern yourself, these thoughts take over. As you mull over and over again your remembered "sins," they take on a life of their own and grow until they seem mountainous to you. My problem is that they are only molehills that I refuse to make into the mountains that you perceive. Coming from two such distinct positions, there is nothing that I can ever do that will really clear up the situation. I know that I fail you. My prayer is that somehow the God of love and forgiveness will give me the wisdom to restore your sense of wholeness and holiness. I do not want you to fear the other side of life. I want your death to be a joyous recognition that you were a good and faithful servant.

I love you,
Audrey

Jesus

Dear Mother,

I know that your faith has always been such an important and real part of your life. You have depended on prayer and have found reassurance in your belief. It really saddens me that it has now taken such a weird turn. It's peculiar, too, that it is not something that we can share as we talk together, for your delusional views are so very real. I guess even this is part of your faith stance in this time and place.

I do not know how to cope with your telling me that Jesus has been at the nursing facility. He spends a great deal of time there and is a constant source of help to your imaginary friend, Frances/Marian. The idea that really knocked me for a loop was when you told me that Frances had been flown away to a new home in the plane that Jesus was piloting. When I sought to find out where the plane was kept, you informed me that he had a special airfield and continually used it to get away from people. You were so happy that Jesus had been available to help your friend (whom, incidentally, I was not able to help).

Jesus, at a later time, also was the person responsible for setting up a care routine for Frances. When I offered to find a way to see that she received the attention she needed, you proceeded to call to Jesus rather loudly. I was more than a little embarrassed as you sat in the lobby, paging him on the network that only you can hear. There have been many occasions when Jesus was involved in your fantasy life.

You never seem to see anything incongruous about the fact that this is 1995 and Jesus lived 2,000 years ago. It would seem to indicate a deep trust and strong belief system that even in your delusional behavior you turn to Christ as the answer. I have no need to disillusion you, but I do wonder if this will always be a helpful hallucination, or if it has within it the seeds of a loss of faith. I was told by one of your nurses that you were terribly distraught and walking down the hallway muttering the name "Jesus" at the time you fell and broke your arm. There have been so many difficult ramifications of that fall that I have not been able to discuss this with you. I do not know what I could say, even if we were to talk about it. I do not want to diminish your trust level in Jesus, and if this is a source of strength, then I guess it does no harm. Is this Jesus in the nursing home a new way for you to feel connected to your religious beliefs? There is no way for me to determine just how much reliance you place on these hallucinations, so I will just have to find some way to be affirming of this.

I love you,
Audrey

Jesus and Your Faith System

Dear Mother,

In writing this letter to you, I recognize how Jesus, your faith, your belief in God, and your needs that are influenced by your unreality are all tied together. In the early days of hallucinations, you were terribly concerned that you could not pray, that you could not reach God. I remember your talking of a dry spell in which you could not focus on prayer. This was a most traumatic time for you, and there was nothing I could do to give you confidence and trust in God. Putting this together with your "sin" and inability to find forgiveness, you were sure you had lost your way. So many burdens weighed heavily on your heart.

Faith and trust in God have been all-important in your life. Discussions about faith have been one of those areas in which we could always have meaningful conversations. So much of what I learned about spiritual experiences first came from you and our home life. I am certain that if you could hear what you say now you would be absolutely astounded, and perhaps it would make you a little indignant, if you were more lucid.

I guess that personalizing Jesus as part of the nursing home is one of the ways in which you have moved from the dry spell into a sense of close companionship with your God. Since you can't seem to pray anymore, having Jesus in close proximity may be your way of living in communion with God. I am not sure about the theological basis for these ideas, but if it means that you have found a way to live more happily, then I praise God.

Do you really have a belief system anymore, or are these ideas and concerns so mixed up with unreality that you can never find a way to get back on track? What this means for me is difficult to say, since I am certain that none of my answers will be acceptable. Life seems to be full of questions and no clear answers.

I love you,
Audrey

ACQUIRED LEARNINGS FROM MOTHER'S MENTAL LOSS

- Personality changes exponentially when loss of sensory perception causes a person to have hallucinations and dementia.

- Tense and prickly relationships, new and more difficult to deal with situations, are the order of the day. Lack of trust and unbelief about the real world make life difficult for the caregiver.

- The pathway for the days and months ahead stretches out with no way of determining where it will lead, if anywhere, and with no viable or happy ending. There will be days and months fraught with tension, the expectation of difficulty, and a sense of defeat.

- Problems have a dailiness about them that may overwhelm both the parent and the caregiver. It is difficult to try to explain things to a person who may have had small strokes and whose memory has become impaired. Connections between ideas and information become so easily confused in the mind of a person with dementia.

- A strong religious faith may have served over the years as a bulwark against hopelessness but in these later years may become a source of anxiety and judgment. Since the caregiver cannot enter into the disjointed realm of perception, it becomes impossible to then turn faith back into the sustaining life force it should still be.

- All the gamut of emotions is part of the experience of dealing with a mentally confused person. For the caregiver there may also be feelings of guilt. There is, however, the possibility that all the pain may be an avenue to new insight, new strength gained, and perhaps a way that leads to calm acceptance and serenity for the caregiver.

- There is little hope that the aging parent can find easy or calm acceptance. If the caregiver can learn how to deal compassionately with the unreality, then there may be hope for the person to find some joy throughout these last years.

Letters to My Mother about the Etceteras of Life

Lord, I've had it,
Up to here.
A crisis I can cope with.
But the everlasting picayune frustrations
are driving me out of my mind.

A crisis I could grapple with.
If I lost my leg, I think I could adjust
with some nobility, too.
But what's noble about a corn on my little toe?
What's challenging about a cold that hangs on
and on and on?

The faucet drips, Lord.
That kid forgot his books again.
It is impossible to get everything clean at once
because while I am ironing, the wash piles up.
I've had it—and had it.

I wish you had called me to a grand task,
a clear-cut and noble endeavor,
instead of the frustrations of my day.

Which is what I am called to—
called to pray while the faucet drips,
called to priest to my neighbor while my corn hurts,
called to fix faucets

and to maintain the sense of humor that realizes
I am not all that far behind on my ironing—
I'm just ahead on my washing!
It is a matter of perspective.
In perspective, frustrations are little things.
I can cope.
    Amen.[19]

Thinking about Those Things That Don't Fall into Neat Categories

Information on deafness, blindness, physical disabilities, and dementia is readily found in a variety of sources. There is not only the published word but also much oral tradition as people share their stories in intimate gatherings. Sometimes the spoken word takes on an almost "can you top this?" but on other occasions valuable information and insights speak in welcome tones to the needs and concerns associated with specific difficulties. A caring cadre of people may help to ease our unease with disease.

Along the way, however, we come upon a group of concerns that have no physical or mental ramifications. Or maybe they do have impact on already existing conditions. There is no appropriate name for them. They are the "etceteras" that end a long list of other disabilities. These "etceteras" cannot easily be encapsulated in one overarching term. They are little bits and pieces of flotsam and jetsam that keep bumping up against the person or persons struggling to stay afloat. They are like time-release capsules, released not all at once, but piecemeal throughout a given twenty-four-hour period. Unlike the medical time-release dosages, they do not make one feel better, but rather they act as irritants until one wishes they had never heard the word "etcetera."

The "etceteras" are the little niggling annoyances that in and of themselves, on an individual basis, do not demand fixing or coping with, or, for the most part, acknowledging. Throughout one's lifetime the "etceteras" are frequently glossed over and forgotten. In a relationship with an elderly parent with many disabilities, the "etceteras" can play a major role. The "etceteras" may be a two-way street for both the disabled and the caregiver. What started as a tiny itch, a small bit of annoyance on the part of one, can take over all of that person's energies and cause a major eruption, and the interaction between the child/parent and parent/child is forever altered. Such an interaction evokes a response followed by another response and the need to justify oneself. An "etcetera" may be sloughed off or it may become a "cause célèbre." The participants in the story carry responsibility for what will happen.

Anger and Love

Dear Mother,

I end all of my letters with "I love you," and if I reflect on it, I realize it is basically true. There are some times I have been with you, however, when love is not my dominant emotion—sometimes it is frustration, sometimes anger, sometimes close to plain dislike. When I think about it even more, I realize that all of those emotions and feelings can be contained within love. If they are, I can truthfully say, "I love you."

When I experience this kind of anger, I frequently wish that I could shake you or tell you off. When that wish overtakes me, I have to realize that telling you off would mean speaking loudly, being overheard and misunderstood, having other people think I am mean and uncaring. It's hard to maintain your anger when you have to repeat your wrath in the same sentences that have already been misunderstood. I know that my feelings must be subjugated, so I bottle it all up and go home and vent my annoyance on my husband. It is so unfair.

There are times, I am certain, when what you feel about me may not be love. Since I often have to make decisions for you that are not what you want, since I have to try to persuade you that you are experiencing hallucinations, plus a plethora of other ways in which I frustrate and anger you, I am certain that you do not always feel loving toward me nor understand my love for you. I wonder if you, too, have periods when you would just like to hit me over the head and tell me off, or if, even in the midst of your anger, you still recognize my caring concern.

Far too often incidents in which we almost come to verbal blows are fraught with misunderstood words and your adamant statements from your dementia. I have no power at times like these when your perceptions are grounded in your own reality and not in what is actually happening. We go around and around, with your stubbornness increasing and my annoyance being exacerbated, and we come to a stalemate. Your words "Let's not discuss this anymore" are not helpful, for we both go away with a sense of incompleteness and unfinished business. Out of these times I go away not only with pent-up feelings of anger, but also, more importantly, with remorse that trying to put you in touch with reality may have demeaned you. For me this is most traumatic, and I am not certain just where that leaves you, but I am fearful that it means more diminishing of your sense of worth, of your being a whole person. I think I need to spell out for myself those ways that I show my love for you, so that I may look at them and see if there are more meaningful ways that I might respond in our times together. When I try to think through these caring connections, they sound so limited, as if there is really very little I do, and yet I know that these tasks absorb a lot of my time and energy. Why do I believe that it isn't enough? Is this my fault, or is this a subtle message that you send me, and is it at times not so subtle? It is difficult to define love in any meaningful way for someone who cannot see the loving concern, who cannot hear the words spoken in love, who retreats into her own world of inner reality that does not allow me a place. I am saddened and I can only end this letter as I do all my others,

I love you,
Audrey

Hugs, Smiles, Caresses

Dear Mother,

It was nice being with you today. You seemed to hear me, and we were able to carry on a limited conversation. When I sit with you, either outdoors or inside, I try to make it a point to sit on your better hearing side so that our being together can be meaningful. Our visits are so often limited by your inabilities that we seldom seem to have any fun; you are the one who has always suggested that we should have more fun.

I have missed seeing your happy smile—you just don't do much smiling anymore. Some time ago I told you that you needed to practice smiling. I even gave you some tactile hints of what you needed to do by lifting the corners of your mouth. We practiced several times the first day I suggested it. Now almost every time I see you, I ask, "Have you practiced smiling?" If you do not understand the question, all I need to do is push up the corners of your mouth. This almost always results in a smile.

Once in a while you tell me that you haven't practiced because there is nothing to smile about. Then I must think with you of some of the good things in your life that would make you want to be happy. That is really a difficult thing to do these days. Your imaginary friend, Frances/Marian, often does something requiring help and then you cannot smile. I know that smiling is still part of you, since my friends who see you at the nursing home tell me what a lovely smile you have. You always did have that, along with a gleam in your eye. I miss those spontaneous smiles and gleams!

When it seems that no smiles will be forthcoming, I resort to tickling you and you are oh, so ticklish. For the few moments in which I do that I feel we are making contact on a very primal level, and I hope that it speaks to you of loving and nearness and care.

Some of my caresses and hugs come as I keep my arm around you and attempt to help you sit upright, not tipped over to the side. I want you to feel that I am there for you. I wish I knew if that is what you feel, or if it is just something that you put up with. There is a certain aloofness, separateness, especially when you tilt away from me to the left. While I do not take this as an attempt to be apart from me and recognize it as part of your physical deterioration, it does have the effect of keeping us as two individuals and not as people whose lives have interacted and been interwoven for so many years. Do the hugs, caresses, and kisses—tactile as they are—speak to you meaningfully?

I remember reading in *The Long Term Care Quality Letter* some words that verbalize my wish for you. They are:

"Children deserve to grow up in a smiling world," said Gerhard Frost. Old and frail people deserve to live there too—in a world that gives them the best of what we have...Old and frail people deserve to live in a world that gives them the best in friendship, listening, humor, and reminiscing. They, like the rest of us, need to be surrounded with love; perhaps even more so in a nursing home.[20]

In a world in which you can't see or even hear too well, how does one communicate a "smiling world"? I realize that smiling, hugging, patting your hand, giving you a kiss are just about all that we have to share. Do these make a "smiling world"? I wish that you could tell me. I want my hugs, caresses, and patting to say
I love you,
Audrey

Only through Me

Dear Mother,
The nurses have such difficulty with you because you will not tell them your needs for medication, for help with dressing, with any other problems that arise. You doubt their capacity to do what is needed or that they will do it on your timetable, so all problems and concerns can be presented only through me. I am not certain what causes

this—is it your dementia, or fear of asking for too much, or what? I think some of it has to do with your feeling that you ought to be able to do it yourself. You have always been a person who used your willpower to accomplish extraordinary feats. Is this part of your self-discipline?

Numbers of your problems fit into the "only through me" category. Hearing aid concerns, even simple things like replacing a battery, require a call to me. Your call, with its demand that I come over immediately to take care of the problem, leads to feelings of annoyance when it is such a simple thing as moving up the volume, which any nurse could do. Your need for help in dressing is another disaster area, because if you call on the nurses for assistance you expect that they should do it at the moment you want it done. I know how much you value your independence and being able to care for yourself, but you make it difficult for others to help you because you assume your schedule is the only one there is.

I am really at a loss to understand your reluctance to assume that the nursing staff, who work with such a variety of human needs among the other residents, could not take care of you as well. I know that they ask if they can help, but you say that you must talk with me. Then, you complain to me because you do not get the help, and there am I caught in the middle again, trying to ask for assistance that I know you will refuse because the timing is off. That phrase "only through me" is all about being caught in the middle.

Being in the middle is an unpleasant place to be, since I try to balance your requests, concerns, and demands with what can be expected of the nursing staff. I do not want to be seen as a cantankerous daughter among those people with whom I maintain other relationships. I do not want you to see me as someone who does not care, who does not do the very best to make these years as good as possible. That phrase means very little to you who suffer from so many debilitating physical ailments. I recognize the futility of trying to make life viable for you. It seems that there is no good, there is only getting through each day. "Only through me" makes life difficult indeed!

I love you,
Audrey

Control

Dear Mother,

In many of my letters to you I have mentioned your need for control that was always an important part of your life. You thought a thing through and determined the way you felt would be best, and then you tried to manipulate people and events to fit that pattern. Now there are such a few ways left in which you can have a sense of control that losing it must be a devastating thing.

Most of my memories show you as the person in charge. At home you were the more dominant. For the most part, all of us fell in with your plans. You had such an amazing ability to see the whole picture and be able to visualize what needed to be done to make the picture fit our family's reality. You were not always on target, and sometimes, individually or collectively, we disagreed with you and asked you to look at other possibilities—and sometimes we succeeded. Even in those situations, some-how the final result seemed to be under your control.

In groups outside the home you rose to positions of leadership in which you exercised control. Neither I nor others experienced this control as domination or tyranny, but all had a sense that you were in charge. Concern for people, diplomacy, and true friendliness informed all your leadership tasks.

Even in your years of lessened hearing, even with your dependence on others to allow you to be included in social events, you still found ways of taking control. If you could initiate the conversation, then you would be a par-ticipant. It certainly was understandable, but our conver-sation oftentimes would be limited by this factor.

I am not certain that you consciously sought for power and control. It may have been merely a by-product of your capability in such a diverse number of areas. Now disabled in multiple ways, you cannot exercise that control. I wonder what happens inside you when that which has been such a key part of personality is taken away. Is it possible to sublimate this need, and what does it do to your image of yourself as a whole person?

I suspect that of all that life has dealt you, the cruelest blow is your powerlessness—your loss of all control. It must damage your pride that I am the one to decide on just about everything in your life. It must be demeaning. Caring for you means that I must take over because you cannot control matters on your own. Is there some way in which I can give you the belief that you are not a pawn to be moved around the chessboard of your advancing years, but a person who, even now, controls some decisions? I have tried to give you that power, but find, then, you are unable to make a decision—no matter how unimportant it may be. It is so confusing to try to determine what helps and what adds to negative feelings.

I do not know whether control and power are passed on through the genes, but as I ponder this desire to be in charge of oneself, I look at myself and wonder about my taking control of your life at this point. Do I have a need to be in charge? I am aware of how much aggravation there is in my life when you will not go along with what I have determined is best for you. I do not always consider *your* best, but what will be easiest for me. Too often I am only feeling my own needs and desires, my rights in the retirement years of my life, and I allow these to cloud my caring for you. All these ambiguities about control get mixed up in my mind, and then, in the confusion, I find no clear directions.

I wish there were a way to converse about these matters so that each of us could achieve workable answers about our relationship. I know that the one-way street of my asking the questions and giving answers that may or may not reflect you is inane. I want you to believe that you matter, and I want to find wholeness for myself.

I love you,
Audrey

Seeing Doctors

Dear Mother,

I have been in attendance in your early retirement years and even in these latter years as you visited such a variety of doctors, specialists, and persons in the health professions: the hearing specialist; the retinal specialist who informed you of your advanced macular degeneration; the neurologist who tried to alleviate your concerns about your terrible visions; the psychiatrist who did all kinds of tests that ascertained that your delusions and paranoia were the result of sensory deprivation; all of them confirmed that these were aging problems and that there was only minimal help available—bad news for you.

In addition, there were the trips to the urologist, the gastroenterologist, the orthopedic specialist, the podiatrist, the dermatologist, and the general practitioner. Your visits for X-rays, MRI scans, and to emergency rooms have been a regular part of my life as we have dealt with the multitude of your illnesses. I have hours and hours of time credited to my good Samaritan account.

It seems impossible to think that so many hours could lead only to deep disappointment and a sense that life would continue on a downhill spiral. I sort of feel like Sisyphus who was continually pushing that rock uphill, only to have it roll down to the bottom again—an endless labor of frustration. So many of the visits were like starting up the hill again—and again—and again. That was true for me and even more so for you. However, your unwillingness to accept that this was as far as you could go demanded repeated visits to many of these doctors, always with the same results—devastation for you and the belief that I should try harder to find solutions.

I have to admit I grew weary. I grew resentful of the fact that you kept putting me in the position of never being able to find an answer that was satisfactory to you. Acceptance of the inevitable was never part of your nature, and I guess you thought it should not be of mine. Perhaps I was, and am, too willing to settle for less than your answers, but I have learned that there is a limit to my willingness to pursue unattainable goals for you. These twilight years are unhappy ones for you, and there are no new pathways to explore. I do not want to continue to push the rock uphill. I have visited the doctors and the emergency rooms, and now I want to make you comfortable, to try to find the means of giving you happy moments, and to love you just the way you are at this time. Will I be able to communicate this to you, heart to heart, since there is no other language in which I can say these words?

I love you,
Audrey

Helping Others

Dear Mother,

Just the other day I was reading a book that so perfectly described you that I wanted to share it with you:

> Human beings find pleasure in caring for others...Frail people need to be cared for, but we must remember that they also need to give care. Being of use, being able to give as well as receive care, makes being in need an easier burden to bear. Cognitive impairment limits the demented resident's ability to take care of others, but it does not erase the need. Helplessness is a dangerous, debilitating condition that can even be fatal. We must learn how to prevent its development and reverse its course.[21]

Your need of being a helper is so great that even in the nursing home you try to find ways of assisting others. Since you cannot take care of real people where you are living, you have found your own unique way to meet this need in the person of Sandy/Lottie/Frances/Marian. I am not certain how I personally can prevent or reverse this process, but I sure wish I knew because perhaps then we could get rid of your imaginary friend. It is an anathema to me!

So many of my letters to you seem to be filled with my wishes and desires. My wish in this letter would be that you would see some need to care for *me*. This answer would be beneficial to both of us. You could be indulging your need to give care to others, and it would make you less cranky and crotchety with me.

Your change of personality since your disabilities have taken over is almost unreal. From being a loving, caring, happy person, and a delight to be with you have changed into a demanding, unhappy, and—let's face it, at times very disagreeable—person, but generally only with me. To all the rest of the world you turn a very pleasant side. I would love to have you show me this side of yourself.

I do understand that you are not aware of this. If I mention this aspect of your persona, you inform me that you always try to be nice. Conscientiously you apologize to me when we have a little tension, but not because you think you have been at fault. I know that you are trying to do what you have done all your life—smooth out the stormy areas, but without ever having to deal with the root causes. Unfortunately, you are not cognizant that the root causes are all a result of your disabilities. Since we are powerless to be able to have the loving conversation that would truly eradicate the problem area, the end result is that we are both unhappy.

It is nice that we can identify the need you have to help others; it is devastating to know that there are no real answers for this in your handicapped position. I tried through activities such as planting a small flower garden, but you gave it up; by means of friendly conversations with others, but you cannot hear them. That's it! I feel like a failure and so do you.

I love you,
Audrey

Money Matters

Dear Mother,

Some of my greatest challenges come when you and I have to discuss money. For the last eight years I have had to be responsible for taking care of your money: I am a cosigner on your accounts, I balance the checkbook, I write all the checks, I take care of your needs as they arise. Even though I do all those things, you still seem to doubt my ability to handle the money wisely. I wish I could just forget this activity altogether.

One good thing that has happened lately is that increasingly you have given up demanding an explanation of the amount of money on hand. Now you have turned to another way of making money a major concern.

The petty cash account is a case in point. Your particular health center allows residents to place money into a petty cash account. When you entered the nursing facility, we carefully opened such an account, telling you that it was there for your use. This is not a source of comfort, because you are certain that you will not be able to get the money out when needed. I am not sure, at this point, that you have the capability to recall that it is there or how to go about having it made available. If I mention this account at the times you are asking me for money, you write it off as if it were nonexistent.

A second case in point relates to your belief that you need to have money on hand "in case." This is very hard for me since the health center does not want its residents to keep money because of the possibility of theft. I have tried and tried to explain that you have no need of money while you are there, and since you only go out with family members, we pay for any items purchased. Does the lack of tangible money give you the feeling that you have been abandoned?

I keep trying to find out what the "in cases" are. They are never very clear in your mind, but the need to have $5 or $10 is terribly real. I know that the Depression years left their mark on you and recognize that the availability

105

of ready cash acts like a security blanket for you. Perhaps this is the only means by which you feel you control doing something special for yourself. Equally real, though, is the lack of need or your ability to be in any place where that money will be used. I am always there when you go out.

Nevertheless, knowing how important the money is to you, I give in and make certain that you have a few dollars in your purse. I cannot continue to fight a battle against your unreal thoughts, and I recognize that it is a small price for your sense of security—even though you will not use it. I guess if someone steals it, I will just re-place it again because you seem so fearful that without money you will not be able to control some strange, "what-if" events. You are so confused and have so many fears that I do not need to add others.

Money is frequently needed by Frances/Marian for food or clothing. It is always a conundrum to me to know how to deal with the money that you want to give her. I have to find some way to take responsibility for getting it to her since; otherwise you will just sit in panic waiting for her arrival. The day that you wanted me to drive you to meet Frances in order to give her $5 for food was a time to be remembered. You thought I could just drive up and down the streets of the city until we came upon her, since you were unclear about where she was located.

After a good half hour of working out where you thought it was, you agreed to let me deliver the money to her. While there was no such delivery, I gave you strong assurances that Frances/Marian was greatly relieved to get the money. The amazing part of all that was that you accepted what I said and believed me. So often it doesn't work out that way.

The trifling amounts are not that significant, but I guess I treat them as if they were. Maybe the lesson is just to do what you want and not worry about the rest. Money is only a thing, but *you*, you are important.

I love you,
Audrey

A Guilt Trip

Dear Mother,

Your situation is more than difficult; it is one that I am not certain I could face. You feel so put upon, so abused, and then you take out that resentment on me. You use several phrases that I just hate to hear. They act on me as a catalyst to guilt. I guess I don't want to think that you consciously try to make me feel guilty because of my inability to resolve your situation. The difficulty is that these remarkable phrases act like a knife turning in an open wound that seldom gets a chance to heal. I hear them often, and I absorb them into myself. I do not blame you for my willingness to take on this guilt—that is my problem. I do wish that you could expunge these phrases from your vocabulary.

The first phrase goes like this: *"I know you are doing what you think best."* Implicit in that statement is the assumption that it really is not best and that I am not meeting your needs in any way. Again we get caught up with your unreality and my reality, and in this case there is nothing that I can do that will satisfy you.

A second phrase is: *"Sometimes you make me feel like nothing."* I don't know what that means to you, but it says to me that even when I try to make you understand what is happening in the real world and I cannot make the kinds of changes you want, at some level all I communicate is that you are of no value. I am not certain just what words or actions of mine lead you to that conclusion. My load of guilt increases to a very high level because I know that I have tried so hard, and there are no acceptable answers.

"Why do you have to go away so much?" is another phrase that makes me think I am being selfish because I am not there for you. The problem is that I have other obligations—to my husband, children, grandchildren, myself. Trying to balance these requests, demands, and needs means someone gets shortchanged. You must take your turn at being on the short end.

Way back even before I retired, I recall your saying that you didn't want to be a problem because we as a family deserved times of rest, relaxation, and periods for discovering who we are individually. Those memories seem to be gone for you and your self-absorption has become so great that you look on my being away as a repudiation of your needs. I look out for you by making all the necessary arrangements for companionship and leaving numbers where I may be reached. Even when I do that, do I feel guilt? Yes, I do. Do I need to make changes in my schedule? No, but I do need to give up the guilt.

No matter how well I plan ahead, how carefully I consider your needs, how much I give you of my time and attention, it never seems to be enough. Too often I end up feeling ashamed that I cannot do more. The circular pattern of your words, my taking on the guilt, and the feeling of frustration has to be broken. I need to say, "No more." The guilt trip is an endless road to nothingness.

If you were to read this letter, you would deny my statements. In fact, I know I could not send it; I would tear it up. My guilt, my problem, my decision.

I love you,
Audrey

Not Taking Enough Time

Dear Mother,

Today we tried to deal with one of your frequent requests that your drawers and closet need to be organized. This is an activity that you believe must be done several times a year. This is something that I know you would like to have me do *with* you, and I would prefer to do it *for* you. In my mind this activity should take about fifteen minutes of my time. Your closet is really very small! Imagine my chagrin when I discovered that you think this should be almost a full day's activity. So much for my decision to do it posthaste.

Even when I make time for this, we come at it from two such divergent points of view. It seems to me that the only arrangement that is satisfactory is the one you suggest and that involves your sense of organization. Your solution is for me to lay all the clothes out on the bed and let you go through them piecemeal, thus taking up a great deal of time. The really sad thing is that you do not understand what it is that you want to happen. You cannot see the clothes and have no respect for what I tell you about the them. You are indecisive, and then you forget exactly how you want to arrange the clothes, and we spend a tedious hour in fruitless activity. On the other hand, if I attempt to do the job myself, you complain that you cannot find anything because I don't spend enough time orienting you to the locations. You end up feeling upset that I don't give enough time to your project, and I just want to say, "Forget it, I have other things to do." Time is the culprit.

The feeling of lack of accomplishment is one that I live with daily because of your demands for more time. If the giving of more time to these bursts of activity ever led to satisfaction on your part, it might seem worthwhile to do the tasks over and over and over again. I wonder how I can make this innocuous, oft-repeated activity into something that will make you believe that you are accomplishing your desired ends, without taking more of my time. How do I assure you that the time I can give is more than enough to do the task? The problem, as I see it, is that we are at two different points. You want me to meet your criteria of the use of my time. I want to find some way to deal with your ineptitude at completing any project in a satisfactory way. There seems to be no way to achieve balance as I struggle to give you the necessary time and find fulfillment for myself. We both end up in total frustration over an activity that is not worthy of the expenditure of so much energy.

As I approach, with a degree of dread, your requests for time to do your tasks, I recognize that you sense time in boring minutes, and I fill mine to overflowing with commitments to many other tasks. Even though I willingly share my time on a daily basis and even try to make for the extended periods of time that you desire, I sense that I never have done enough. If I confronted you with this, I know that you would say I do more than enough, but it is your delusional mind that demands more than I can give of time and effort. Maybe I just need to acknowledge that I cannot please and continue trying to do my best.

I love you,
Audrey

Journaling My Insights II

Our dim eyes seek a beacon,
And our weary feet a guide,
And our hearts of all life's mystery
Seek a meaning and a key[22]

To Die

So many times I have heard Mother wish that her life would end. She feels as if there is nothing left for her, and yet, with her strong belief that God has a purpose for everyone, she has determined that God must still have a plan for her. She tells me that she does not understand what it could be in her deprived world, but her faith seems to sustain her. Fortunately or unfortunately, her physical health seems to be so good that it looks as if life will continue for yet a while. There will be no heroic life-sustaining measures taken to maintain her life. She is totally ready to write finis to her life. All of us in the family concur with her wishes.

I was asked the other day by a doctor whom she was seeing how I felt about this death wish. It made me really stop to think just what it is that I would hope for her. My answer was a strong affirming "yes" that she be spared additional losses with which she could not cope. My "yes" acknowledged that death might be preferable to spending much more of her life in the silence and the darkness of a world filled with weird hallucinations and terrible paranoia.

Even with my "yes" comes the recognition that I desire that she may go simply and easily into that new world where pain may be no more. I have to believe that in God's eternal kingdom she will find light and music and joy that will counteract all the years of disabled living. I know that I will rejoice for her that she has finished the course.

What Happens after Mother's Death?

The question of Mother's dying raised for me the need to reflect on my feelings when she will no longer be with me. I know those years will free up significant amounts of my time. I need to start developing a lifestyle that will sustain me through all the changes of these latter years of my life.

Mother's dying will be a time for me to look back and remember not only the years of her being a cognitive, creative, loving human being, but probably even more importantly, the years of disability and trauma and overwhelming concern. Will I be able to overlook the problems and frustrations and value them as the years of more intimate, closer contact? Will I recognize the difference between the years of giving care and the world of being mature adults together?

I have written about the changing child/parent to parent/child relationship that has been ours. I shall have to begin to look at her life as being all of one piece, since she has still been *Mother* even with the changes that have been brought about by her disabilities. She is and will be in my memory the mother who cared and gave me the opportunity to be the caregiver. I shall miss this particular caregiver part of my life. I will miss her, but I can rejoice that she no longer will need my erratic, sometimes angry, sometimes frustrated, sometimes even unloving care. I certainly would like to feel I do not need to criticize myself because there were things I left undone. I hope that in her dying I can know that my love sustained her through her life. I want to be able to celebrate all the years of her life.

Where Do I Go from Here?

Where have all my letters and journaling led me? I recognize the need for tying up loose ends, thinking through what is demanded. There are bits and pieces that need to be put together in order to gain clear insight. I recognize that there are two distinct sides to this equation: finding meaningful, valuable tasks to enhance my personal needs in the here and now, and acting as caregiver for my mother, as long as she lives.

As I look at the caregiver side, I want to try to make life seem good for Mother. I want to make her feel that life has some validity for her right now. I want to give Mother warmth, love, and feelings of worthwhileness, even as a disabled person. I would like to present some real solutions and not just come up with unsatisfying placebos for those almost impossible situations she faces on a regular basis.

As I look at the personal side, I am confronted with the fact that in the core of my being is real pain for my inadequacy and selfishness. I must learn how to live free from guilt about my inability to make things better for my mother. I need to be able to step back and accept my need for independence, recognizing that it is a good and necessary thing for me to do.

It's as if there is a pivotal point, such as one finds on a seesaw, where the balance is just right. When I recognize this, then I must try to shore up that central spot so that life can have its ups and downs for both of us. If it is possible to do this, and I have some doubts about my ability to separate myself from overloading the caring end, then perhaps I will have achieved a greater degree of independence for both of us. Will my opening up my world to new vistas help to broaden Mother's horizons? The disparity between the caregiver and the personal need almost seems like two opposites, making me feel as if I am caught on the horns of a dilemma.

In church one Sunday the minister talked about the Greek word *thaumaturge*. He conveyed its meaning as "a miracle worker," but then went on to add that it meant to *empower us to do more than we think we can.* I really have no ability to be a miracle worker. I am mostly a "get the task done" kind of person who can envision the way things might be and attempt to make them happen. As I pondered that word and its meaning, I saw *thaumaturge* as a possible way to tie up some of the loose ends with which I have been struggling. Perhaps I can be empowered to do more than I think I can.

I am not sure just what that empowerment would allow me to do, but I do know that I want to get out of the no-man's-land that keeps me filled with stress and the desire to flee from such rigorous demands. Perhaps a miracle can occur.

Trying for Perspective

My journaling has led me to try to put all of my thoughts into some kind of perspective and come to conclusions. I need to be about the business of finding my own perspective, biased as it is by being terribly subjective and influenced by my own sense of impotence. Perspective, in and of itself, is such an interesting phenomenon because it depends so much on the position from which one views a thing.

> The developmental biologist R. Davenport has stated that we are capable of knowing something only because differences or contrasts arise. Because it takes at least two things to make a difference or to form a contrast, one of which is our own psyche, it follows that we are in some sense responsible for what we call "reality."[23]

How my reality informs the perspective from which I look at what has happenened and is happening in two lives may make it very different from what the casual observer sees. From my point of view, my impotence to find solutions, whether good or bad, is only descriptive of my very human inadequacy. Even with all the ponderings, deliberations, and times of serious reflection, my perspective still indicates only *my* point of view. In the great scheme of life, I recognize that these musings, these attempts to find answers are only a small ripple in the vastness of a world awash in trauma. There are so many people with far greater problems, there are so many persons who have the capability of finding answers; I need to recognize the insignificance of just one struggling human being.

There is still the most important perspective—that of a God who sees the whole of creation and yet cares for each person, creature, flower. Where is that perspective reflected in this diary/journal? It isn't! I need to find some way to look beyond my turning, churning thoughts. One morning recently I came across a verse of scripture found in Isaiah 44:24–25. It opened up a whole new concept and allowed me to see beyond my own pettiness.

> Thus says the LORD, your Redeemer…
> who turns back the wise,
> and makes their knowledge foolish.

Those words gave me great courage—my knowledge, or even my lack of knowledge, may be foolish. I need to turn in trust to the One whose perspective is all encompassing and who sees the little lives of Mother and myself in their entirety. I cannot know, I cannot fathom or plumb the depths of God's plan, but if I am wise, I can admit that if I look for God's perspective, I may find wholeness for both Mother and myself. All of my letters and journal entries seem to be so bound up in pity, needs, sorrows, lack of patience, and other human conditions that I have not allowed myself to let go and trust in God's loving providence. I have probably failed Mother by not helping her to open up her life to the glory that can come as God's love flows through her. I want to help her experience that love as it flows through me. First, however, I must allow the fresh winds of God's grace to permeate my whole being and find renewal so that I may meet the challenges that each day brings.

Will my consideration of God's perspective change me? Will I be able to find answers? I don't know! I can only hope that I may find a new perspective that will work for both of us. I do love my mother. I do care that she should know overflowing love and not that which is given stingily. I want to rejoice and open my arms wide to all that life has to offer of pain and happiness, of love and life-giving joy. I want to do that as I parent my parent who gave me so many of the lessons of my life. May God help me to be a singer of hymns of joy even in the confines of a care community.

As I began to think of hymns of joy that I might sing, I was reminded again of the letter I wrote about the mystery that was so deep that it was unexplainable, and it called to mind a hymn that has become meaningful to me. It contains the line: "From the past will come the future; What it holds, a mystery." Then in the words that follow comes an answer with which I can live and which explains so well what God's perspective is. The entire hymn is a joy-filled answer that gives me a sense of peace and serenity. Here are its words:

Hymn of Promise

In the bulb there is a flower;
in the seed, an appletree,

in cocoons, a hidden promise;
butterflies will soon be free.

In the cold and snow of winter
there's a spring that waits to be

unrevealed until its season,
something God alone can see.

There's a song in every silence,
seeking word and melody;

there's a dawn in every darkness
bringing hope to you and me.

From the past will come the future;
What it holds, a mystery

unrevealed until its season,
something God alone can see.

In our end is our beginning;
in our time, infinity;

in our doubt there is believing;
in our life, eternity.

In our death, a resurrection;
at the last, a victory

unrevealed until its season,
something God alone can see.[24]

This hymn really spells out my mother's problems—
the silence, the darkness, the loneliness of winter—and it
offers hope that in its season, God will bring new
opportunities. I do not need to know the answers, I do not
need to anguish over those matters about which I can do
nothing, nor do I need to fill my life with feelings of
"ought." It is all there in the constant refrain of the *Hymn
of Promise*: "unrevealed until its season, something God
alone can see." I want to trust in God's perspective; this I
need to do. I must learn to wait quietly and patiently for
"the season" to be revealed. I hope it will be my victory
and Mother's, as well, as we accept God's perspective.

On Mother's Death

Mother slipped away today at ninety-one years of age.
She developed pneumonia, and it was too much for her
system. I found myself spending the best part of several
days with her. Mostly I held her hand and let her know
that I loved her. She moved into a coma, and the last two
days were a time of releasing her to eternity. We held a

memorial service for her, and all of her grandchildren sent letters sharing what she had meant in their lives. From those moments I received the gift of knowing her again as a vital, loving woman who was so outgoing.

I shared my final tribute to my mother at her service:

> I want to celebrate my mother's life, all of it, not just the loving person who taught me about living, about God, about values and service, but the person she became when her deafness and blindness left her isolated in her own world. That changed her from being a person in control of her life into a different person who had great needs. In this latter category she offered me the opportunity to become a caregiver. I hope that, even in her confused state, she knew she was loved. I celebrate the moments in which we had fun together, in which we tried to make sense out of her nonsense.
>
> It is important to me to celebrate also the wonderful woman she was in her whole person. Mother was a caring, loving person who was concerned about and acted to alleviate injustice. She was a creative, vital woman who had talents she shared with all. She was a friend to so many people.
>
> Her faith and her church life were the mainstays of her life. More important to me, however, was her way of making her family into a cohesive unity. What all of us learned from her was love and caring for one another. Her grandchildren loved her for her sense of fun and her caring.
>
> I celebrate the creative years of her life and ministry among us. I celebrate all the years she was with us and rejoice with her that she is at peace and able to live in whatever eternity opens up for her.
>
> Mother, we rejoice because you lived!

Afterword

"Afterwords" are those last words that give an author one more opportunity to try to share one last thought, one final word that puts the book into a desired perspective. I did not want this book to end on anything other than an upbeat note. I want to think that I have offered the possibility of hopefulness in it. I want to believe that coming through the multiplicity of words there is the promise of resurrection. The trauma of sharing myself and my mother's story, warts and all, may open up for others the possibility of finding new life even amidst the difficulties that threaten like storm clouds on a sunny day. I know that life continued for the two of us, not without other times of stress, but perhaps in brighter hues as I sought new pathways created out of the storms of life.

This book indicates that there have been many storms that have affected these two people as they have passed through changing roles and learned new ways to relate to one another. There has been a look at what has happened as the storms have shaken the relationship between these two people. While there have been negative effects on the two participants, there also have been learnings that those same storms have scattered new seeds and offered the opportunity for the development of new life even within the soil of the old relationships. May this book make you the recipient of some of the seeds that have been scattered as you have journeyed through these letters. Perhaps these words will act as a promise that new life may be found if there is trust in God's way with life.

Notes

[1]Jo Carr and Imogene Sorley, *Bless This Mess and Other Prayers* (Nashville: Abingdon Press, 1969), 34.

[2]Jan Coombs, *Living with the Disabled: You Can Help* (New York: Sterling Publishing, 1984), 78.

[3]Rainer Maria Rilke, in Larry Dossey, *Healing Words* (San Francisco: Harper, 1993), 21–22.

[4]Ibid., 18.

[5]Gertrude Stein, in Dossey, *Healing Words*, 18.

[6]William H. Thomas, *The Eden Alternative: Nature, Hope and Nursing Homes* (Columbia, Mo.: University of Missouri, 1994), 70.

[7]Ibid., 21.

[8]Coombs, 78–79, 81.

[9]Ibid., 71.

[10]Thomas, 21.

[11]Robert Browning, "The Common Problem," in Thomas Curtis Clarke, ed., *1,000 Quotable Poems* (Chicago: Willett Clark and Co., 1937).

[12]Hazel Nowell Ailor, "Gift" in Grana, *Images in Transition* (Nashville, The Upper Room, 1976), 90.

[13]Helen Hunt Jackson, "Spinning," in Clarke, *1,000 Quotable Poems.*

[14]Frederick Lawrence Knowles, "My Faith," in Clarke, *1,000 Quotable Poems.*

[15]Edwin Markham, "The Man with the Hoe," in Clarke, *1000 Quotable Poems.*

[16]Coombs, 74.

[17]*Thomas*, 28–29.

[18]James Kenny and Stephen Spicer, *Elder Care: Coping with Late-Life Crisis* (Buffalo: Prometheus Books, 1970), 56–57.

[19]Carr and Sorley, 39.

[20]Brown University, *Long Term Care: Quality Letter*, vol. 6, no. 21, (November 14, 1994), 7.

[21]Thomas, 28–29.

[22]Author unknown, "Our Dim Eyes Seek a Beacon," in Clarke, *1,000 Quotable Poems.*

[23]Dossey, *Healing Words* (San Francisco: Harper, 1993), 68.

[24]Natalie Sleeth, "Hymn of Promise," © 1986 Hope Publishing Co. *Chalice Hymnal*, (St. Louis, Mo.: Chalice Press, 1995), no. 638.

Index of Letter Topics